What other reade
*Heaven's Secret of Success*

"This is a comprehensive, insightful and powerful teaching of how to embrace the matters of life that lead to spiritual maturity, while avoiding the hindrances that keep you from a victorious harvest as a child of God. This book will move you to a higher level of intimacy with God as you learn His custom-designed will and destiny for each of His children."

Charles G. Tucker
*President, Tree of Life Ministries, International*

"An incredible guide with keys to help you move forward in doing what God has called you to do, along with how to identify what is keeping you stuck in unproductive living. This book is a treasure of encouragement for helping you to achieve God's full purposes for your life. A must read!"

Alisa Burns
*Founder, Women of Increase*

"Going through this book has really kick-started me to move forward in my personal life and calling. Thanks!"

Julie Peace
*Graphic Artist*

# HEAVEN'S
# SECRET OF SUCCESS

Cultivating Your Identity from Seed to Harvest

## J. Nicole Williamson

*King's Lantern Publishing*

Printed in the United States of America
Lightning Source
www.lightningsource.com


Library of Congress Control Number: 2011915730
ISBN-10 0615532853
ISBN-13 978-0-615-53285-1


Quotes used with permission.

Unless otherwise indicated, Scripture quotations are taken from the New
American Standard Bible ®, Copyright © 1960, 1962, 1963, 1968, 1971, 1972,
1973, 1975, 1977, 1995 by the Lockman Foundation. Used with permission.
(www.Lockman.org)

Interior Design by Kathrine Tripp
Cover Design by Constance Woods, www.streamsofmercyart.com
Illustrations by Julie Peace
Photo Portrait by Bethany Eileen Williamson
Editing by George K. Williamson

www.kingslantern.com

# Dedication

To Daniel and Bethany—may you live, laugh, and love life to the fullest as you journey into a divine destiny with God, discovering each day the joyful depths of who He is and who you are in Him. May your spirit rise on wings as you take hold of your God-given identity, natural and spiritual, and soar with Jesus into the purposes of the Father by the power of the Spirit. May you teach your children to do the same. Remember always, you are loved.

# Acknowledgements

Thanks to my wonderful husband, Ken, for your constant support and expertise in editing. Thanks to Kathrine, Constance, and Julie for your help in making this book a masterpiece. Thanks to Bethany for your photo work, and Daniel for your continual support. Thanks to Dr. Wilhelmus and the staff at Eye-Care Texas—with special acknowledgement to Kelly, Tiffany, Leslie, and Evelyn—for your support of my work to get this book written and the time needed to do so. Thanks to everyone who has encouraged me along the way.

# Contents

# INTRODUCTION

*"As long as the earth remains, seedtime
and harvest . . . shall not cease.
. . . Sow with a view to righteousness."*
— *The Holy Bible*

A ll my life I have had a sense of destiny, and with it a longing to fulfill it—a pull of passion to participate with God in His grand purposes with His creation. Even as a child, I felt God calling me, perhaps not with an audible voice, but with an inner voice— one that awakened my heart with desire to know Him intimately, and be fruitful in His Kingdom.

Throughout life, however, I have discovered that such fruitfulness has its enemies: the bondages of a self-centered soul, dark spirits that seek to prevent divine purpose, religious traditions that chain the mind, and cultural "norms" that influence the heart away from God. I have experienced them all, and am still learning the Way of Light that frees me from their destructive influence.

I love how God's Word reveals so many aspects of His nature: Creator, Father, Healer, Redeemer. In this book, however, I want to emphasize the aspect of God as the Divine Gardener. Scripture says that He sows His Word like seed in the soil of people's hearts;

He sows with the vision of a harvest in our life. Indeed, with the vision of a harvest in the whole earth—a harvest of mature sons and daughters of His own likeness. He says that the Word He sows will not return to Him empty (*fruitless*), but will accomplish what He sends it to do. And the work that He begins in us, He will finish (Phil. 1:6). It's a promise, a promise that has a process....and predators that seek to stop its fulfillment.

To grow as Abba Father's child, I have discovered that it means that I, too, must become a gardener, joining Him as a co-laborer for the harvest He desires in my life, and in the place where He plants me. We often say that the mind is the place of the battlefield between good and dark thoughts, but Scripture says that thoughts proceed from the heart. Thus, it is the *heart* that is the ultimate battlefield within mankind. Interestingly enough, the heart is also a garden—uniquely designated by God to be His dwelling place. In my own heart, I have seen the rage of darkness give way to the triumph of Light where losses become wins, and impossibilities turn to possibilities with God. I have known many battles in my garden, but I am growing continually in knowing who God is, and who I am in Him.

Scripture clearly shows us that our time on earth is about one special thing—the harvest of God's purpose with mankind—with us. All creation itself manifests His purpose—from the *planting of seed*, to its manifest *resurrection* that grows with life, to its resulting *fruitful harvest.* In the Old Testament, God commanded His people, Israel, to celebrate three specific feasts every year that commemorated this process: the *Feast of Unleavened Bread,* the

*Feast of Weeks,* and the *Feast of Ingathering* (also known as the *Feast of Tabernacles* or *Booths*). These, He said, are *"My feasts"* (Lev. 23). Why? Because these three specifically speak of the journey of a seed that is buried, rises with life, and bears fruit. These are a picture of Christ, the Seed that would be *buried, rise again* and bring forth a *harvest* of sons and daughters of God.

The *Feast of Unleavened Bread* speaks of the **sacrifice of Christ** on the cross as the Passover Lamb; the *Feast of Weeks,* celebrated at Pentecost, speaks of the *firstfruits* of **Christ risen;** and the *Feast of Tabernacles* speaks of the full harvest of those who *"tabernacle with God".*

A people who dwell with Him is what God is laboring for. And these dynamics—the *law of sacrifice* (cross), the *Spirit of holiness and triumph* (resurrection), and *intimacy with God* (tabernacle) — are what nurture such a people to be successful in the purpose of God with fruit that glorifies Him. And all these divine dynamics operate by one key: the love of God.

From Genesis to Revelation, God's plan began with His Word— His voice that ignited life on earth, life that will one day culminate in a great harvest. But first, the harvest begins in your life and mine, as we grow in our God-given identity—both spiritual and natural— through the power of the cross and resurrection, and intimacy with Him.

Jesus said that Father is looking for those who will worship Him in spirit and in truth, that is, those who will love Him with all their heart, soul, mind, and strength. It is this kind of love that is willing to be crucified with the Son, be raised to new life by the Spirit, and press on to know Him—to bear fruit that glorifies Father, and make ourselves ready, as a *holy Bride*, for the Son.

God desires the fruit of His harvest in our life. Will we engage with His voice, His Word, and let it produce all that He has sent it to accomplish?

Time is short.

I pray that the following pages will impart fresh vision for your successful and fruitful journey as God's child—that the seed within you sees its full harvest. May the words you read give deeper understanding regarding the principle of sacrifice and Spirit of holiness that triumphs to transform your life, crown you with victory, and glorify the Father in heaven.

It is a true statement that what we sow is what we will reap.

**"Sow with a view to righteousness"** (Hos. 10:12).

# 1

## GOD PLANS FOR A HARVEST

*"....bring My sons from afar, and My daughters from the
ends of the earth, everyone who is called by My name,
and whom I have created for My glory,
whom I have formed, even whom I have made."*
*—God (Isaiah 43:6b, 7)*

God brought mankind into existence, not out of a random act of creativity, but with a divine plan. People—you and I—are not a happenstance, coincidence, accident, or "oops". We are a manifestation of divine thought. Before creation began, God had a positive notion in mind: you and me. He wanted a family, loving children in His image that would grow as sons and daughters of His likeness. Why? Because God loves relationship.

At creation, God brought forth myriad forms of life—each one having within it the seed for the next generation of its kind. From that point, He established that offspring of any kind would begin life as a seed, a tiny time capsule of DNA that develops to maturity through a favorable environment. It is no different for the children of God. God formed mankind from earth's ground, creating them as male and female after His own likeness, with seed inside them for the next generation. However, mankind was different from the rest of creation; they had an identity that went beyond "natural". Their lungs were filled with God's breath. They had intimate fellowship with God. And for the development of His supernaturally natural children, God placed them in a garden with a work to do. Here, His presence was the atmosphere in which they would mature and multiply as His ruling offspring—as governors of the earth.

And so it began—this wonderful thing called people in the image of God.

While this seems like a simple beginning, the truth is that God's purposes are much bigger than the two paragraphs in which I just framed it—much bigger than countless volumes could contain—as big, I'm sure, as eternity itself. So to give a better, deeper perspective into the heart of God regarding this grand event of mankind's creation, I want to share a story, a conversation . . . an imagined dialogue. God Himself uses parables to teach us spiritual truths, since illustrated lessons often convey truth better than explanation.

Since we know that creation was planned with forethought, the following is an imaginary conversation about what God's own musing within Himself—the Father, Son, and Holy Spirit—might have looked like during the planning stages for mankind. Now, no one really knows exactly how the dialogue went, but perhaps it went something like this.

**Father:** "Hmm. Tell the angels to quiet their music just a bit. I'm thinking. . . I have an idea."

Jesus waves His hand to hush the angels in the throne room.

**Son:** "What Father?"

Looking at the Holy Spirit and the Son, the light within the Father glows more brilliantly than ever.

**Father:** "What if We create a different kind of being from anything else We've created so far—different from the seraphim and cherubim, or even the archangels . . . a creation in Our own likeness—offspring."

Jesus leans back to recover a bit from the surprising thought.

**Son:** "In Our own likeness? You mean, like, *children*?"

**Holy Spirit:** "It's a wild idea for sure!"

Father, continuing His thought . . .

**Father:** "Yes! And they will join Us in ruling over things We create—they can sit with Us on the throne."

**Holy Spirit:** "On the throne with Us? Now wait a minute."

At this the Son and Holy Spirit rise, and pace, as they ponder Father's words.

**Son:** "Now Father, We know how created beings can be . . . treacherous. Just look at Lucifer and how he deceived a third of the angels who had to be vanquished from Our presence. What if they betray us, too? How can We dare trust anything created again, and with such an intimate position with Us? I don't know about this."

**Father:** "But think about how delightful it would be to have sons and daughters."

**Holy Spirit:** "Hmm . . . yes, a delightful thought."

**Son:** "Dad, do you think it's possible? Would they . . . could they love Us as We love each other? Would they love one another? Could they be—*family* together, *and* with Us?"

**Father:** "What do you think, Holy Spirit?"

**Holy Spirit:** "All things are possible when true love governs the heart."

The Son's brow furrows.

**Son:** "And what if they fail? Like Lucifer?"

**Father:** "That's a very good question, Son. What if they do?"

**Son:** "We could give them a list, a set of rules to follow. But what will keep them, you know, on board, on the straight-and-narrow, in harmony with Us?"

Father, shaking His head . . .

**Father:** "I don't want robots. Rules alone make robots. They have to have choice—freewill. Like We have choice."

**Holy Spirit:** "Okay, I'll say it again—LOVE! I will be with them and pour Our love into them."

**Son:** "Yes! Great idea Holy Spirit, after all, who can resist love?"

**Father:** "Ha! Yes, who can resist love? We will create a world over which they will have dominion—they will rule it. We will be with them, and they will have Our nature of goodness, gentleness, mercy, love, faithfulness . . . of holiness. They will fill the earth with more sons and daughters in Our likeness—enjoying life, designing, building, inventing—interacting with the holy unseen realm together with the realm of three dimensional matter."

**Holy Spirit:** "I will be their Teacher!"

**Son:** "I will train them in their identity!"

The Holy Three-in-One looked at one another and cheered, "Children!"

**Father:** "Communion with Us will illumine their heart and mind so they can govern a dark world with the presence of Light."

**Son:** "Uhm, what do you mean, a 'dark world'?"

**Father:** "Not all the angels stayed with Us. Nor will all mankind because of their choices. Lucifer will be there, luring them away from Us as he did with so many angels. Some will follow him, listening to his lies, choosing to live in darkness instead of in Our Light."

**Holy Spirit:** "Then this task of raising sons and daughters will not be so simple?"

**Father:** "Not quite. There will be a fall because of a foe, and a flood because of rampant folly, but then will come a family from someone whom history will remember as Our *friend*. We will parent this family as our own. We will love them deeply and give them Our words. And yes, we will give them family "rules" about how to love Us and one another."

**Son:** "I thought You didn't want to give them rules."

**Father:** "Our laws will be written to teach them Our heart. Truth will be hidden inside Our words for the one who seeks and desires truth. But the words themselves will not keep their heart in relationship with Us. Only love can do that . . . only love that lifts the letters from print on paper to write it upon the heart. But many of this family will also will fall away, though some will follow Us. Others will have a mere form of godliness. But all this will be preparation, the precursor to the great heart of My plan, out of which will come a great harvest of true children in all the earth."

**Son:** "What is that Father? What is the heart of Your plan?"

The Father turns to Jesus, looking deeply, lovingly, into His eyes.

**Father:** "You, Son. You are the heart of My plan."

**Holy Spirit:** "Go on. We are listening."

**Father:** "No matter how many words we may give them, mankind's spirit that will die at the fall will still be dead. It must be revived. That is why rules will only make them religious, not children in Our likeness. They will be slaves in darkness. We must redeem them, purchase them back from their bondage in sin. But first, the payment of their redemption must be paid."

**Holy Spirit:** "How is that to be done?"

**Father:** "The payment of sin will be death. Blood must be spilled to pay their penalty . . . the blood of one who is sinless. Or they cannot be rescued from eternal death."

**Son:** "But no one on earth will be sinless because of the sin nature released in all people at the fall, no matter how good they try to be!"

**Father:** "You are right."

**Son:** "Oh, I see. WE will have to rescue them. They won't be able to rescue themselves."

**Father:** "Right again."

**Son:** "And how are WE going to do this?"

**Father:** "You, Son, will become one of them, but You will be hated by the very ones We created out of delight. You will face the terror of darkness, but Your reward will be great. You will have no easy task in this, Son. You will be the Seed buried in the earth itself, as well as in the soil of people's hearts—of those who receive You. From Your sacrifice will come the harvest of holy children."

**Holy Spirit:** "And those who reject Him?"

**Father:** "They will, because of their choices, become another harvest. Will You do this, Son?"

Jesus looks at the sea of glass beneath His feet, and then back at Father.

**Son:** "I cannot do this alone."

**Holy Spirit:** "I will be with You!"

**Father:** "We will all be together—I will be in You on earth, and You will be in Me, and Holy Spirit will be together with Us, too. As always."

**Son:** "Then, yes, I will go. I will become one of them. And I will be the Seed buried and raised for a harvest of children in Our image. Holy Spirit and I will show them Your ways, Father. We will bring them to You. We will do this together."

**Holy Spirit:** "Well, then, are We ready?"

**All Three:** "Let's go!"

## THE CREATION AND THE FALL

And so God created the heavens and the earth, making man and woman in His image and establishing them as governors of the earth realm. And yes, they did fail, even though they lived in a favorable—no—a perfect environment. They turned from God to follow Satan's voice; you know how the story goes, how that voice led them to eat from the tree of the knowledge of good and evil. It was, and still is, a tree whose fruit carries the DNA of sin that misses the mark of intimacy with God.

Adam and Eve disconnected from the Source of Life and connected with a voice that echoes sound, but does not edify or energize with life. And so their journey entered a crisis—their separation from Light changed their identity and altered their destiny as a reign of spiritual darkness was unleashed on the earth. Fruitfulness was exchanged for pain, sweat, and thorns. Success in the divine purpose for their life was strangled.

God, however, was not surprised. He never is, you know. And though He had to remove them from the garden of His presence, He did not abandon them, but clothed them with animal skin, shedding the blood of an innocent animal on their behalf. It was a picture of the Son who would one day come and shed His innocent blood on our behalf, in payment of *our* sin.

We see from the fall, that it is not a perfect circumstance that creates a favorable environment to mature us as God's children, but it is the condition of the heart and *how* it connects with the voice of God that nurtures the seed of divine identity within us, or not.

## THE REDEMPTION

Undaunted in His love, Father God was persistent in His intent to have children in His image. And in His appointed time, He sent the Son to pay the penalty for *all* our sin, not just Adam and Eve's. Jesus' work on the cross and His resurrection opened heaven's portal of redemption, making mankind free to come out of the darkness and breathe new life in the Light—like children who have finally come home. At the cross, the Father planted His Holy Seed in the earth in order to have a harvest of holy sons and daughters. There, He removed the curse and restored to mankind an identity as fruitful dominion bearers who govern earth's realm. There, at the cross with Christ, is where our journey begins as God's children.

God's harvest basket is now being wonderfully filled, but there is more fruit that He desires. Souls have yet to be saved. Destinies have yet to be defined. And gifts have yet to be realized and cultivated, in your life and mine. The great harvest time is coming, actually two harvests—one of the righteous who will be gathered to the Father, and the other of the "tares of wickedness" who will be gathered and cast into eternal fire.

The Apostle Paul, inspired of God, painted a picture of what the two seeds will look like in their mature state at full harvest time. Here's what he said about the seed of sin: **"For men shall be lovers of their own selves, covetous, boasters, proud, blasphemers, disobedient to parents, unthankful, unholy, without natural** affection, trucebreakers, false accusers, incontinent [without self-control], fierce, despisers of those that are good, traitors, heady, highminded, lovers of pleasures more than lovers of God; having a form of godliness, but denying the power thereof: from such turn away" (2 Tim. 3:1-5).

That seed with an earth-destroying nature will create "perilous times". But Paul also taught how the seed of God, planted in the heart and cultivated, will look completely different than the seed of sin. As these mature, they will look just like the Son—bringing healing to the nations through their anointing and gifts (we will look more at this in the next chapter). Instead of "perilous times," they will create an atmosphere of "times of refreshing".

What seed will you carry to maturity?

Paul also spoke of a prize of the *high calling* of God for those who embrace the Son (Phil. 3:14). In Greek, the word "high calling" means: heavenly invitation to a feast. What feast? The final Feast of Ingathering, the harvest, also known as the marriage supper of the Lamb. The *"prize"* signifies the crown of reward given to the holy children who are at that feast—crowns that will be thrown at Christ's feet in gesture to say, "YOU are the One worthy of this crown because of Your sacrifice for us!"

## A RETURN TO GOD

Father God set His plan in motion with only one means of His harvest coming to full fruition, to full stature—*relationship* with Himself through the Son by the Spirit. Jesus Himself, when on earth, grew not just physically, but in wisdom and inward "stature" (Luke 2:52). In Hebrew, the word *"stature"* means to be *"of age"*. It means to be responsible for one's own action regarding what has been taught through the Torah (Word of God). It means being a productive member of the community. In fact, the Hebrew ceremony that celebrates this wonderful passage of maturity involves reading from the Word of God and leading in prayer.

Did you hear that?

Connection with the Word and intimacy with God grows us to full stature! This is not a call to know the letter of the law, but to connect with the voice of God. It is the responsibility of love: **"You shall love the Lord your God with all your heart, and with all your soul, and with all your mind, and with all your strength"** (Mark 12:30). Divine love is what matures God's harvest in us. It is what conforms us to the image of Christ and prepares us for an eternal reign with Him. This is God's desire from the beginning.

Satan still roams the earth speaking, deceiving, devouring, and drawing people away from the Light. The battle we face since the fall is the war of voices—who will we listen to? God or the devil? The Holy Spirit or the spirit of the world? The voice of Christ or self?

**"You did not choose Me but I chose you, and appointed you that you would go and bear fruit, and that your fruit would remain"** —Jesus (John 15:16a).

God's plan hasn't changed since the beginning. He wants holy sons and daughters. And guess what? He still has a garden where He walks with them—with us! No, it's not in Eden. It's found in the heart that receives and believes His voice. Here is where God deposits His Word to begin its journey of growing us up in Him.

23

The question is: what is the favorable ambient we will give it? Will His Word be *successful* on its journey in our life? Will we meet with God in the garden? Or are we busy conversing with another?

God has a unique plan for each of our lives; a plan of success as His unique child. Come with me, and let's discover what that plan looks like and how it can be successfully achieved in our life.

# 2

## SUCCESS BEGINS WITH A SEED

*"Listen to this! Behold, the sower went out to sow."*
*—Jesus (Mark 4:3)*

Success. How we love its melodic sound, sweet taste, and the satisfying feeling it gives us! It is the gratifying achievement of hard work and sacrifice for something longed for, something planned for. It is the applause of fulfilled intention, the cheer of having arrived at a long journey's end.

We love success not only in ourselves, but in others. We stand in ovation to those we see overcome obstacles through great struggle to attain some impossible dream or lofty vision. We identify with their struggle and their triumph inspires us to think that perhaps we, too, can conquer the difficulties that stand between us and a desired goal. But to experience success, we must understand its story, its journey. We must take into account the point from which it begins—its origin—as well as its voyage and arrival.

If you get right down to it, we were created to be successful people. We were formed in the image of a "successful" Creator.

Can we not say that God is successful? Of course we can! After all, is He not the Triumphant One who attains His goals in spite of opposition? Yes! So what does it mean for *us* to be "successful"? What is the goal and what is the opposition?

The world tells us that success is about fame and fortune. That it's about wealth. But God says that *authentic* (what comes from the *Author*) success is being conformed to the likeness of His Son.

**"For those whom He foreknew, He also predestined to become conformed to the image of His Son, so that He would be the firstborn among many brethren"** (Rom. 8:29).

In a sense, the Creator's definition of true success is not so different than the world's concept: in Christ we have the greatest fame of all—being known by God, and we have the greatest wealth of all—the unlimited blessings in Christ as we sit with Him in heavenly places. Oh, if we could but grasp what we have in Him!

So what are the *obstacles* to achieving such success? Well, we can start with an agreement with the spirit of the world, cultural lies, and strongholds. These are all the devil's schemes—these are obstacles to the seed of God's voice flourishing in our life. They strangle our heart, corrupt our soul, and darken the mind. They stifle spiritual gifts and manipulate natural talents, altering our true identity and stealing our harvest.

So what is the *key* to overcome and succeed in the purpose that God has for us? Jesus! He is the key and model of authentic success for *all* mankind. We were *all* created to be God's fruitful children as we are conformed to the image of His Son . . . though not everyone accepts and follows this magnificent divine plan.

## BEGINNING THE JOURNEY

Now, the success of anything begins with a seed—whether a biological seed, a philosophical seed or a seed of faith. Inside that tiny seed is a **hidden *code* (DNA) that determines what that seed will look like when it becomes mature.** The seed contains a *blueprint* for its destiny. And the seed's most simple intention is to grow up—to mature and bear fruit that carries more seed for a new generation of its kind.

This is the "law" of nature put in place by the Creator—the One who made good seed, both natural and spiritual. He not only formed and ignited natural life, but has put eternity in the heart of every person, giving each a measure, a seed, of faith (Eccles. 3:11; Rom. 12:3).

The destiny that God planned for each of us rolled into motion one day when a human seed (full of possibilities and capacities) awakened with life—ignited by a tiny sperm that fought its way, relentless against all odds, so that we could exist. The sperm was opposed but triumphant, carrying with it a host of unique qualities, physical attributes, intellectual capacities, emotions and personality, and individual abilities. The two together (the human seed and sperm) united to become a beautiful creation: a human being.

All seeds begin their journey in a secret place—buried in soil, embedded in a womb, lodged in a mind, implanted in a heart. Success begins with the *law of sacrifice*—where something of worth is buried and allowed to go through a separation ("death") process. Here, separation experiences multiplication for growth.

Each seed carries a specific DNA to its identity, so that an acorn becomes an Oak tree (not a blue jay); an apple seed becomes an apple tree (not a lemon tree); and the seed of a lion becomes a lion (not an ant). You are a human being because you came from the living seed of a human being . . . not a fish, reptile, or ape. Each seed carries a blueprint of qualities that develop and mature through *favorable environments*.

Now for mankind, our physical and psychological attributes represent only part of the DNA we are given. As humans (being different from the plant and animal kingdoms), we have an added dimension: we have a *spiritual* DNA: we are body, soul, and spirit. Our spiritual DNA is either: 1) spiritually dead and walking in darkness, apart from God, or 2) spiritually alive through new birth in Christ, walking in light and fellowship with the Father, Son, and Holy Spirit—connected with the voice of God.

**". . . It is written, 'Man shall not live on bread alone, but on every word that proceeds out of the mouth of God'"** —Jesus (Matt. 4:4)

## HUMANS—NATURAL AND SPIRITUAL SEED BANKS

Now for me, my spirit came to life when I was seven years old. A school friend invited me to her house to participate in an after-school Bible club. There, her mother told me the gospel story. I believed what she said, I received the word of truth, and I asked Jesus to come into my heart. It was very simple. After that, I was aware of God's presence in a new way. I wanted to know Him more. And though I was a little child, I had a sense of destiny, of purpose, that I could not explain except that it had to do with God and me, and the world. My young mind understood in a simple way that Jesus gave

His life for me, and now He wanted me to give my life to Him. This is the *law of sacrifice*—where I choose to be crucified with Him.

Just as with a seed in nature, the Word of God that I received (and continue to receive) has a journey inside me. As I give it a nurturing environment in my life, I see it manifest in the Spirit of holiness and a *triumphant spirit* of life and power. The DNA of God's voice continually causes me to grow and mature in Christ-likeness—enabling me to overcome adversities, push back opposition, and conquer enemies that try to hinder my development.

As children of God, we grow naturally and spiritually according to the DNA of the Holy Seed within us. He is the Triumphant One, Liberator, Joyful One, Prince of Peace, Healer, Restorer and Rebuilder. He is the Divine Seed that transforms us from living as mere men and women, so that we experience life as anointed sons and daughters of God in every way.

**The nature of Christ is our new nature—liberated, peaceful, joyful, and triumphant. As He is, so are we.** The Divine Seed inside a child of God has a nature that cannot be contained in its fire of desire to be fruitful for the Father, and to restore a fallen earth. The life of the Seed wants to manifest through our uniqueness in personality, talents and gifts. And yet, like I said, the journey of development is not on a bed of roses, but on a battlefield—a battle for our heart. Only as we are willing to be buried with Christ and die to self, does His life begin to be released inside us, extending both downward as "roots" in God, and upward into the light as "branches" with fruit that nurtures others.

29

We see that the whole life of a seed is a journey of release. It begins with a hand that releases the tiny form into the earth at planting, and from there it continues a release (of growth) in height, dimension, and extension. The stem and leaves release oxygen, the extended branches provide shade, and its fruit releases nutrients into the mouth of those who eat it. Its whole life is about releasing, giving, and not holding back or shrinking back. **Such release of life reveals the heart of the Creator.**

## THE JOURNEY OF LIFE

In nature, a seed's *germination* (the awakening of life) can be ignited by water, fire, or even the vibration of music (as science proves). As development continues, that little seedling grows upward, searching for the light. Meanwhile, its roots go deep, seeking water. This process of seeking light and water continues in the plant all the way till harvest. At that point, the baby seed from the matured fruit (that either falls to the ground or is gathered at harvest) will be planted to commence its own identical journey as its parent.

In our modern world of technology, it's easy to forget the experience of a seed's journey, of caring for it until it produces a desired harvest. You know, it's called "gardening". Remember? My grandmother was a skilled gardener. She even canned her own food until she was ninety-three years old. I go to the grocery store for my food. I also can't keep *any* plant alive at my house (well, I might have had one once). All the plants in my home are plastic. I don't have to water them, fertilize them, spray them, prune them or talk to them. I don't have to invest any time for them to look great, though I do occasionally dust them. However, they do not produce fruit. They do not produce more plants. They are a sterile mockery to the real world—a false representation of true life. They look good on the outside, but they are seedless, dead . . . but they make my house look nice.

## DESTINIES ARE THE HARVEST OF CULTIVATED SEEDS

Okay, I know you get the picture by now, but I'm laying an important foundation for keys that will unlock your understanding to fulfill the anointed destiny that God has for you—one that glorifies Him. Let's look at the seed journey another way: a destiny, simply put, is the harvest that results from nurturing the DNA of who you are, both naturally and spiritually. For this to succeed, you must know the elements of who you are. A lot of people don't know who they are. I meet people in my line of work every day who can't tell me what are their passions, gifts or spiritual calling.

This is a problem!

**Jesus knew who He was. He was bold in saying, "I am the Way, the Truth, and the Life. I am the Bread of Life. I am the Light."** We are all familiar with the age old questions: Who am I? Why am I here? Where am I going? Even many Christians know their "title" as being a child of God, and where they are going for eternity, but they really don't know who they are in Him now! What are they supposed to "look like" as the Holy Seed within them grows? I'll give you a clue: it ain't faithful church attendance; it is the likeness of the Son.

Do you know who you are?

Success at anything doesn't just happen. A successful artist doesn't just pop out of their mother's womb with paint and brush in hand. They begin with a seed of desire and God-given talent, and through *practice* and *training* they nurture their creativity to fruitfulness—they give it their time, attention, and their focus. A musician doesn't study the viola if he wants to be a pianist. A successful business person doesn't just "happen" randomly either. They start with an innovative idea that is developed through research, setting goals, creating strategies, investing finances, and disciplined work to bring about planned fruitfulness. And for a child of God who desires to glorify their Father, this whole process begins with time in His presence. He is the One who gives the ideas and strategies needed not only for our success, but to release the authority of His Kingdom for the healing of the earth through our life.

 Likewise, a farmer who wants a crop of corn doesn't throw out any ole' seed, but prepares the ground and plants a specific seed—corn seed. The prophet Hosea told God's people to *"sow with vision for righteousness"*—**to plant with a *specific* harvest in mind.** This is true for any person of any career or industry. We must ask ourselves: what are we sowing? Because *that* is what we are going to reap.

As the children of God, we must ask: **what is the harvest Father desires of our life?** What is the Word He has spoken, or is speaking to us that we are to nurture? What is the DNA He has placed within us—spiritually *and* naturally. What does its mature state look like?

He has a vision for you. What vision do you have for your life—naturally and spiritually?

God envisions a harvest of godly children with divine authority who are intimate with Him, using their anointed gifts and unique abilities for *His* Kingdom. Western Christianity too often emphasizes a type of faith that may not lead a person to godliness, or spiritual authority with power, or even true intimacy with God. Or, it may emphasize godly principles, but leave out divine power. But principles without the presence of God *and* power of the Spirit fall short of the harvest Father desires. We can be devoted to principle (godliness) and have no connection with God's presence and voice whatsoever. But believe me, connecting with God's presence *will* devote us to His ways and principles, too.

The covenant we have in Christ is not only a return to righteousness, but to righteousness through intimacy with God. Good morals are critical to a healthy life and society, but God wants more—He wants children in His image who carry His presence, principles, and power through every area of life and labor!

The Father is looking for a harvest of worshipers—sons and daughters who know His glory, carry His character, and minister by the presence of His Spirit to comfort the brokenhearted, heal the sick, free people from oppression, cast out demons, speak words of hope and blessing, and raise the dead! They do this, not because they are pastors, but because they are Abba's children as they go about their everyday life: business people, military personnel, city workers, and artisans anointed for Father's work in the earth.

I work for a doctor, and often minister and pray for patients as I work with them. One day I spoke a prophetic word of encouragement to a young lady and she asked, "Are you a pastor?"

"No," I replied, "but I *am* a daughter of God."

Some people think we have to be official clergy to hear from God. But every child of God has spiritual ears to hear Him, and an anointing to release life to others—wherever we are, whatever we are doing. It is in our DNA!

Our *spiritual senses* are meant to be just as developed as our *natural senses*, our *spiritual gifts* as well as our *natural talents*— all working together for Father's purposes in, and through, our life.

What does your God-given DNA look like? What are your natural talents? Your spiritual gifts? Do you know? Jesus was a skilled carpenter, anointed teacher, and divine healer. He developed a trade, was skilled in His studies, and was moved with compassion to release the power of the Spirit everywhere He went—from weddings, to picnics, to funerals, to church services.

## THE SEED OF GOD

Jesus was no stranger to a seed's journey. He came to earth as the Seed of God implanted by the Holy Spirit into an earthly womb (Luke 1). He matured as a *natural* son to Mary and as a *spiritual* Son to Father God: **"This is My beloved Son with whom I am well pleased; listen to Him!"** (Matt. 17:5)

Jesus developed naturally *and* spiritually according to His human and divine DNA. He matured in the place of natural family dynamics, developed his natural skills as a carpenter, and grew in wisdom and in favor with God and man—He grew to *full* stature: maturity (Luke 2:52). As a devoted Jew, He passionately studied the Torah—God's Holy Word. As Abba Father's Son, He practiced heart-to-heart relationship with Him through the presence of the Holy Spirit who was His divine Teacher, Comforter, and Helper.

Most of all, Jesus worshipped His Father—loving Him with all His heart, soul, mind and strength, keeping His heart immersed and full of the love of God. His heart was a garden where the rain of God's presence watered the seed of His identity, daily.

Jesus emerged an adult as the express love of God to mankind—a minister of grace with truth on His lips, compassion in His heart, and power in His hands such as the world had never seen. He spoke with heaven's authority that brought the dominion of heaven to earth. He was Son of Man living in the flesh as a true Son to God.

Even His disciples declared of Him: **"To whom shall we go? You have words of eternal life"** (John 6:68).

Now, let's look a little closer at His journey.

## JESUS NURTURED HIS IDENTITY

The DNA of His Heavenly Father coursed through Jesus' blood, carrying with it the blueprint of a heavenly identity, divine authority, and supernatural capacities. He also had the DNA of human flesh from His earthly mother, Mary, and all its attributes. His very cellular make-up contained the DNA of perfect Light and the DNA of fallen mankind—these having opposing mindsets, just like we experience on our journey into Christ-likeness. He had to choose which voice He would nurture—the voice of the Spirit or the voice of the flesh. Which seed (Light or darkness) would He allow to grow in His heart, engage His mind, and flourish in His interactions with people?

35

Jesus went through everything we experience as a human, yet He kept His heart engaged with His Father. He said, **"My food is to do the will of Him who sent Me, and to accomplish His work"** (John 4:34). From early on, Jesus had to learn to dismiss the unjust judgments and opinions of men, and root His thinking in Abba Father's affirmation. He learned to be "family" with God as the abiding presence of the Holy Spirit taught Him to be a Son—an Heir with His Father's nature. He could have sought position, but didn't. He humbly refuted earthly crowns from those who moved with good intentions, but outside the will of God (John 6:15).

He *practiced* listening to Father's instruction, rather than leaning on His own understanding; He depended on the counsel of God in everything, not doing things out of self-effort or striving. He ministered grace, yet was skillful in brandishing truth as a sword against the lies of the devil—against religious spirits that held God's people in captivity (Matt. 4:7; 16:11).

How skillful are we at recognizing the lies that the devil whispers in our ears?

Jesus was not a wimp. He was heaven's humble warrior who nurtured the seed of His identity as Abba's Son through consistent declaration of the Kingdom and His Father's desires. He kept the word of faith in His mouth. He knew who He was. **He knew His identity. He told people, lots of people, "I am the Bread of Life that comes down out of heaven. . . . I am the way, the truth and the life"** (John 6:35).

What is *your* declaration of who you are?

Jesus' thoughts and actions weren't contrary to His identity. He wasn't a *mature* son at birth, but grew in His development as He was *taught* of the Holy Spirit. He paid attention. He practiced a lifestyle of love and faith under the tutelage of the Holy Spirit. He delighted in working with His Father to release heaven on earth, finding deep satisfaction in doing His Father's will.

Fruitfulness for Dad was the harvest He had His eyes on. He never stopped short nor mixed His affections with selfish ambition.

As a human being in relationship with God, Jesus had to *learn* the same discernment that you and I do. He had to recognize the voice of unbelief that whispers in the ear: *what if nothing happens when I pray?* He, too, had to grab hold of vain imaginations and bring them into the light of truth, to successfully battle dark thoughts like: *they'll never accept me.* He had to practice not letting holy anger become fleshly anger, to speak truth with love, even if it meant telling His friend, *"Get behind me, Satan."*

He was divine, but He was also human. And life wasn't served Him on a silver platter. Being a sacrifice for us was a crucible that He *willingly* chose—giving His body to be lashed for our healing, being silent before His false accusers, allowing sinful man to nail His innocent being to a cross for *our* sins. **He did this in love to rescue us from a life of fruitless lostness.** He willingly shed His sinless blood to set us free from an identity in bondage with a destiny of eternal death (John 3:16; Matt. 26:28). He rose from the grave to give us a new identity, one of sonship—an identity with fruitful intimacy with God.

## TRAINED IN THE ARENA OF FAITH

It was the *Holy Spirit* who *trained* Jesus to triumph, teaching Him to break the intruding darkness of the carnal mind by renewing His mind with the Word of truth. Really? Of course He did! That's what the Teacher does . . . He teaches! The *Holy Teacher taught* Him to dismiss the voice of doubt by rehearsing the testimonies of His Father's faithfulness. It is the same for you and me.

Jesus stood strong as a Son, even in the heat of adversity, by showering Himself beneath the rain of the *Spirit — the Comforter's presence*. He fought the battle of faith intelligently, *by the Spirit,* with intent to win in His purpose as God's Son. Father wants the same for us!

How are you letting the Spirit train you in your Christ-like identity?

Are we getting this? Jesus *practiced* nurturing His identity through the presence of the Holy Spirit. He knew what was in His flesh, and so He applied His heart to the way of repentance (turning away from sin and toward Father). He built strong spiritual "triceps" through years of "pumping" truth—lifting it up above the lies of the enemy as the standard of His reality. **He pushed away the spirit of the world by the strength of the Spirit and His worship of One.** He rejected religious mindsets that countered His Father's ways. **He overcame by the Spirit in the arena of life, against the intrinsic folly within His own humanity by continually submitting Himself to God.** He did what He felt the Holy Spirit speak to Him. He loved His Father and hated evil.

He pursued being *skilled* in wisdom, letting His spirit-man rule rather than His flesh.

I think we're seeing the picture by now—Jesus ***practiced*** what He preached and He had a Teacher! The Teacher who is also the Comforter, the Helper. Sons and daughters—children—need teaching *and* comforting.

Jesus doesn't ask us to do something that He Himself didn't do. His power was not super-duper human will-power—but it was the **power of the Holy Spirit** who dwelled in Him, who trained Him in the arena of faith in God, *and* in the understanding of His identity on earth: Son of Man, Son of God—the Word made flesh.

**The seed of God wants to grow inside us, too. It desires a successful journey in the garden of a willing human heart to grow fruit that glorifies the Father.** And what is the purpose of that fruit? The healing of the nations. Our fruit (God's harvest in us) is for the healing of a broken world that desperately needs the restoration of the Spirit by Spirit-filled rulers.

*God, here I am, just as I am. I want to be Your loving child. I give You my life—all of it. Let my heart be Your garden—a place for Your presence. Holy Spirit, make my heart a rich ecosystem for Your truth. Thank You for loving me so completely.*

# 3

# THE SEED OF GOD INSIDE YOU

*"I have been crucified with Christ; and it is no longer*
*I who live, but Christ lives in me; and the life which I now*
*live in the flesh I live by faith in the Son of God, who*
*loved me and gave Himself up for me."*
*—Galatians 2:20*

We've looked at how success begins with a seed—and that authentic success in our life begins with the seed of God's Word being planted  in our heart. But it's not enough to simply know that we have a seed of life sown in our heart, it must be cultivated with *vision*. God, as a Heavenly Gardener, has a vision for the harvest of His seed. He wants us to grasp that vision, too. No gardener is content with simply knowing he has any ole' random seed in his hand, and that once planted, it will *hopefully* develop. No! He has prepared his land for optimal growth of a *specific* crop, knowing what the mature state of his seed is going to look like.

Let's take, for example, a corn seed. The gardener waters the seed, prevents weeds from killing it, and predators from destroying it. Why? Because he envisions himself sitting down to a plate of fresh, hot, sweet, white corn, lightly salted, with sweet cream butter melting down its sides. He imagines sharing this delicious experience with all his family, neighbors, and friends who he invites to his table, too. He knows what he wants, plants accordingly, and waters and guards it consistently. Not ignorantly. Not randomly. But intentionally.

Likewise, some people receive Jesus and accept God's Word, but don't know what the mature state of that seed is supposed to look like in their life. They may think it merely looks like faithful church attendance, being free of apparent bad habits, and a change from vulgar vocabulary. But the life of Christ in us is so much more than what much of post-modern Christianity portrays.

To get a *clear picture* of what the mature state of God's seed in us is to look like, we must look at Jesus—who He is, what He taught, and how He lived on earth. We had a peek of Him in the last chapter, but I want to go deeper. Get a good look. He is who we are maturing to be like. The Father is looking for children in *His* image. Not a religious society.

Vision is critical for the cultivating of a garden. Like us, Jesus had to cultivate the garden of His own heart with vision, to nurture the Father's seed inside Him so that He'd grow in the exact image of His Father. Do you know what the mature state of God's seed— His Word—within *you* looks like? In your character? Your talents? Your gifts? Your relationships?

## WHAT THE MATURE SEED LOOKS LIKE

Let's take a look at the Bible's description of what the mature Seed of God (the Son) looked like as He developed on earth:

The disciples of Jesus hung on His every word. His touch released power. His life radiated love. His words echoed the authority of heaven. This Man's reality was in the power of an unseen Kingdom and a divine presence on earth. The disciples travelled with Him, ministered with Him, experienced His life up-close, first hand. Nothing fake, no hype, no insincerity, and no personal agenda prompted Him. He was the genuine thing, the real McCoy, the Son of God yet Son of Man . . . a Man with a mission. A Man who succeeded in the purposes of God, of whom the prophets spoke of through the ages as One coming to fulfill a divine plan from eternity.

The Seed—the Son—came and lived as the most successful Man on earth, bringing Father the greatest harvest ever—children rescued from the darkness and brought back into light, back into His image to be light bearers themselves.

This most successful Man had one favorite topic to which He gave His entire devotion: His Father's Kingdom, the Kingdom of Heaven. He used myriad parables to describe it to His earthbound, religiously trained, faith-challenged disciples. He taught them openly, privately, on the hill side, in the boat, in the temple, at the table. He spoke revelation through pictures, truth through stories, and demonstrated heaven's nearness with miracles.

He healed blind people, lame people, bleeding and bent over women, men with withered hands. He raised dead sons back to life, including His own best friend, Lazarus. He cast demons out of men and forgave adulteress women, telling them to "sin no more." He cleansed lepers, fed thousands with a few scraps of food, commanded storms winds to cease, turned water into wine and the sea into a walkway. He made fish to jump into fishermen's nets. **And most miraculously of all, He turned boxed-thinking, doubt-**

**ridden, earthly-minded men and women into Spirit-minded children of God who released the authority of heaven on earth!** He trained them to be as He is—ministers of life for the healing of the earth.

Jesus' called Himself the *Vine* and His disciples the *branches* that would bear fruit to glorify Father. They would be leaders—spiritual parents—to future generations of Kingdom sons and daughters, a tribe of *nation-healing light bearers*. Jesus wasn't training them to be followers of a new religion, but to be children who would work with Father in the earth—to do as He did, wherever they went, healing the sick, breaking demonic strongholds, and raising the dead to life.

The disciples' understanding of this was essential. Their "getting it" was critical lest the evil one snatch greatness from their understanding. Greatness? Yes! God's plan for His children—for whosoever will—is so great . . . great destinies with a great identity. How the enemy tries to veil this from us.

Abba Father wants us to know who we are in Him. He wants us to understand the purpose of His work in our lives, and in the earth. Christ-likeness is so much more than how we've viewed it. **It isn't just godly character, but is the maturity of ALL we were created to be, spiritually AND naturally, with anointing, creativity, and divine wisdom.** We may not understand every detail of our journey, but He wants us to know where His Word in us is going—into the full likeness of the Son and our identity in Him.

Okay, we've looked at what the mature Seed looks like. Now we're going to spend a few minutes looking at *His* description of the Kingdom that He came to release on earth for mankind's return to wholeness—a Kingdom now appointed to us.

## THE KINGDOM AND THE SEED OF GOD

The moment that the Father sent the Son to be born a Man on earth, the winds of change began to blow over creation. A new season was at hand—one that would rend the heavens and shift mankind into a new dimension—a return to Father, and a return to *authentic identity.*

The Son ushered in a new paradigm, a new covenant that was no longer for Israel alone, but for all who come to God through *God's Way*—through Christ. The Father established a commission of priesthood that was no longer relegated to one tribe (Levi) in Israel, but to every believer born of God. The seed of God in us— wherever we are, whatever we are doing—is planted in us to grow and release the breath and life of God's dominion on earth.

The Kingdom that Jesus taught and demonstrated is one of a real and present heavenly realm—a dominion of quantum dimension that lives inside you and me as rivers of living waters. It is a realm to be entered and engaged with the simplicity and faith as a child; a realm whose doorway is guarded from the mocking and unbelieving. He said that the Kingdom is not a religious tyranny, but is the power of God to transform mere men and women into spiritual kings and priests . . . a company endued with divine authority.

This company touches a visible creation with the supreme love of an invisible God to edify, restore, heal, and deliver. A company that takes a vehement stance against the realm of darkness led by

Satan who works to crush hearts, steal identity, and kill destinies.

Jesus described His Father's Kingdom as being full of mysteries and supernatural activity, where angels move with the voice of God to help mankind regarding Father's purposes. It holds the wisdom of ancient ways, yet with fresh movement, having keys that give God's children the ability to lock and unlock doors in heaven and on earth. It carries authority to cast out demons, and gives access to heaven's provision for earth's needs.

Jesus instructed His disciples to tell everyone about this Kingdom. Why? Because this realm of the divine, placed in human vessels, is a witness of God to all nations—one that carries an invitation from God for all to come to His banquet table of relationship . . . though not everyone will come. It is a life of sacrifice and selfless surrender to the love of God; a lifestyle of picking up our cross and following Christ; a life crucified with Him yet vibrant with resurrection *power*! It is a life of great reward!

This Kingdom is a walk with the presence of God by the indwelling *Spirit of holiness*, where trust is not put in man or circumstance, but in God's ability to do the impossible—in us, through us, for us, with us. It is an atmosphere that manifests as a flow of inner life that is congruent with God's heart and nature—one that loves what is right in the midst of a world that loves wrong. It carries an inner peace, even when circumstances are turbulent, and joy that continually buoys the heart. It is a realm of unlimited divine blessing given to the poor in spirit (those who are dependent on God, not independent from Him).

Jesus went on to show that in Abba Father's Kingdom, we are

given a special work to do involving our gifts, talents, and dreams. It is a unique work we engage with continual forward momentum, and not looking back. It is a life of unity with God *and* with spiritual brothers and sisters, where the presence of Light is tangible in thought, attitude, and action. **It is not a far-off, out-of-reach, make-believe land, but one that is a present reality with authority over earth's elements and demonic presence that impacts the earth realm.**

It is not a list of rules or powerless words.

Jesus said that it is Father's good pleasure to give this Kingdom to His children, for the call they carry as His ruling offspring in the earth. He taught His disciples to pray, **"Father, Your Kingdom come, Your will be done on earth as it is in heaven."** He heralded the message of the Kingdom together with the call to repentance, that being, a wholehearted return to Father.

All this that Jesus declared is written throughout the gospels of Matthew, Mark, Luke, and John. Read them! They are critical understanding for our identity in Christ. Jesus admonished us, as the children of God, to seek *first* the Kingdom of God before anything else in life. And in so doing, we will find divine supply for every need.

**He that has an ear to hear, let him hear what was just said!**

Don't let these words go over your head or fly past your understanding. If these things are so, then the anointing within every child of God has the authority, like Jesus, to stop earth's storms, feed starving multitudes, break demonic strongholds, and yes, even get needed finances from unseen places (maybe even a fish's mouth like Jesus did).

What does seeking God's Kingdom (and all that His Kingdom provides) mean for you? Your health? Your finances? Your relationships? Your personal well-being? Your career?

We are given a SUPERNATURAL Kingdom. So what are we waiting for? Church to get out?

Yes!

God is waiting for His Church to get out—out of its four walls to engage their identity as the overcoming ones. Overcoming the enemy that deceives them, steals from them and those around them; overcoming spirits of doubt and apathy, and taking their rightful place of authority and work in the harvest field. It's time for the Church to get out—to take her worship to the streets and to the work place. I heard someone recently say: God established what the Church should look like at Pentecost . . . and He didn't do it by putting a steeple on the Upper Room! He sent them out with Kingdom power.

**The question is: will we do what Jesus said and seek first the Kingdom of Heaven to be manifest with divine dominion and provision in every circumstance of life?**

What does that look like for you right now?

## SEEING THE KINGDOM

Jesus taught many things about the Kingdom, yet He declared just *one* of His teachings to be the eye-gate through which the Kingdom could truly be understood in its fullest dimension. He told His students that if they couldn't grasp the truth contained in this one parable, they wouldn't be able to know or comprehend *anything* about the Kingdom.

**"Then Jesus said to them, 'If you can't understand the meaning of this parable, how will you understand all the other parables?'"** (Mark 4:13 NLT)

That parable is Jesus' teaching of the seed and the soil. Why is this one picture key to understanding *everything* else about the Kingdom? Because everything about God's Kingdom on earth has this main purpose: to raise a harvest of children conformed to the image of His Son as the anointed dominion-bearers of the earth. Are you seeing this yet? It's about Him . . . and you!

Let's look at this key parable in Jesus' own words. While it is written in three of the gospels, we are going to look at how Mark shared Jesus' words in Mark 4:3-20:

"Listen to this! Behold, the sower went out to sow; as he was sowing, some seed fell beside the road, and the birds came and ate it up. Other seed fell on the rocky ground where it did not have much soil; and immediately it sprang up because it had no depth of soil. And after the sun had risen, it was scorched; and because it had no root, it withered away. Other seed fell among the thorns, and the thorns came up and choked it, and it yielded no crop. Other seeds fell into the good soil, and as they grew up and increased, they yielded a crop and produced thirty, sixty, and a hundredfold. And He was saying, 'He who has ears to hear let him hear.'"

**At His disciple's request, Jesus went on to explain this parable.**

"The sower sows the word. These are the ones who are beside the road where the word is sown; and when they hear, immediately Satan comes and takes away the word which has been sown in them. In a similar way these are the ones on whom seed was sown on the rocky places who, when they hear the word, immediately receive it with joy; and they have no firm root in themselves, but are only temporary; then, when affliction or persecution arises because of the word, immediately they fall away. And others are the ones on whom seed was sown among the thorns; these are the ones who have heard the word, but the worries of the world, and the deceitfulness of riches, and the desires for other things enter in and choke the word, and it becomes unfruitful. And those are the ones on whom seed was sown on the good soil; and they hear the word and accept it and bear fruit, thirty, sixty, and a hundredfold."

The seed of God's Word was sown, but the *condition of the soil* made all the difference in the world. Only one type of soil enabled the word to see a harvest.

The soil in this parable represents the *condition of the heart.* It is the heart that does, or does not, give favorable growth to the voice of the Lord in our life.

In the Bible, "seed" refers to the Word of God—His **written Word** (the *Logos* of God), His *Living Word* (the Son of God), and His *spoken Word* (the *Rhema* of God). These three have one thing in common: *they are the voice of God.* And His voice communicates His dominion (Luke 8:11; Matt. 7:29). **His voice releases His authority.** The seed of God's voice contains the living DNA that grows us into Christ-likeness; in other words, it transforms us into the image of the *Word!*

## THE SOIL OF OUR HEART

Our Creator is a speaking God—a Father who communicates and a Teacher who articulates with purpose. His communication with us is heard through our spirit-man but processed by the heart, that being, the **throne of our affections, the fountain of our thoughts, and center of our will.** It is our heart that is the environment that is either favorable or unfavorable to the fruitfulness of God's voice in our life.

God couldn't have picked a more apropos setting than the heart—the place most vulnerable to deception and decay, and one most needy—to implant the seed of His life-giving voice.

**"The heart is more deceitful than all else and is desperately sick; who can understand it?"** (Jer. 17:9)

No wonder Father provides a new heart for us through the new covenant in Christ . . . a heart that He washes, restores, heals, and fills with the love of God. He gives us the **heart of the Son**—the most favorable environment to the Father's voice. The heart of the old man—our carnal nature inherent at natural birth—turns away its ear from God, just like Adam and Eve did in the Garden of Eden. That is the heart that is deceitful and corrupt in its self-centered lusts, and what must be buried in baptism with Christ.

**Jesus declared that true knowledge of the Kingdom will stay cloaked in vagueness until we** *understand* **the significance of the journey of God's voice within our heart—from planting to full fruitfulness.** It is a journey that will be attacked by Satan at every turn in an attempt to stop the seed from reaching its full potential in our life.

Are we getting this? This is the essence of what our life in Christ is about: God's Word planted in us, growing us as sons and daughters until, like Christ, we are *His Word made flesh*.

The plot of the story is simple: **Father wants us fruitful; Satan wants us unproductive—stripped of life, trees that never come out of winter . . . a plant that never matures.**

Unfruitful sons and daughters of God mean an unhealed world; fruitful children who know their identity bring healing to their environment. Do not be ignorant of this! We live in a multi-dimensional world beyond what human eyes can see. There are angels all around sent from God to watch and help us and the cloud of witnesses who lived before us cheering us on. But there is also a present demonic host that has one persistent goal: stop the children of men from becoming the fruitful children of God! Darkness wants to destroy.

So here it is—the question we must ask ourselves is: **what experience is God's voice having in my heart and life?** Is it being received? Nurtured? Fruitful? Or is it finding difficulty, dryness, blockages?

## A FAMILY OF GARDENERS

In this parable of the sower, Jesus describes four different types of heart-soil:

1. The soil that is beside the road
2. The soil that is full of rocks
3. The thorn ridden soil
4. The good soil

Obviously, only *one* kind of soil gives favorable growth to the Word of God to bring His seed to harvest.

God doesn't make it rocket science for us to know how to be successful in life—spiritually, naturally, or in any sense. He showed us right from the beginning that nothing could grow until two things happen (Gen. 2:5):

1. God causes it to rain
2. There is a person to cultivate the ground

We have been given the honor of caring for the earth—the earth of our own life, as well as planet earth; a responsibility that cannot be fruitful by our own hands alone, but is a task that requires the presence of God as we join with His desires. When He says that He has given us EVERYTHING we need for life and godliness, He means it! We are not left alone to "figure it out" or labor in vain. He gives us His Spirit and wants us to work with Him.

**And what's more, He will bring others along side us in the work He gives us to do.** He is a Community Gardener! He will bring others into our life to give us the tools we need for our garden, and to align with us in Father's broader garden assignments.

Jesus called His Father a Gardener, a "Husbandman". As the Son of a Gardener, He too lived as a spiritual gardener. As God's children, we are also gardeners. That's the way it is. We are a family of husbandmen.

Now look at this, the word *"husbandman"* carries the picture of one who is married—committed—to the life and destiny of the seed.

The husbandman plants the seed *and* watches over its development (John 15:1). The word *"cultivate"* means to prepare soil for growing crops. In other words, husbandmen—gardeners—cultivate the earth to empower the destiny of a seed. "Guarding" (or keeping) a garden means to be alert against destroyers, whether animals, insects or destructive weeds.

**Gardeners receive seed, sow seed, empower a seed's identity, and protect its destiny from destruction.**

What seed has the Heavenly Husbandman sown in your life? What seed are you empowering and protecting in your life? The seed of God's Word? Or the seed of the spirit of the world? Whatever seed you give a favorable environment to in your heart—that is what will grow. It is the ecosystem of the heart that causes seed to take root and sprout.

**"As the earth brings forth its sprouts, and as a garden causes the things sown in it to spring up"** (Isa. 61:11).

God's children are not fruitless, plastic people like the seedless plastic plants I buy at the store and put in my home. We call such things "artificial". The Bible calls such *people* as "having a form of godliness without power"! Plastic plants don't need soil because they don't grow. They don't reproduce. Real plants needs real soil . . . really good soil. So does the seed of God's Word need really good soil in our heart to grow, multiply, and mature. And it needs a gardener: the Heavenly Gardener and His co-laborers—you and me.

Soil without a gardener will grow any random seed that is carried there by a current of wind, passing fowl, or visiting beast. Without a gardener, the plants overrun each another, are attacked by disease and animals, and are choked by thistles and weeds. Who will help them? Who will help the seed realize its full potential and protect its divine destiny?

The gardener will!

It takes time and wisdom to grow a garden, train a child, raise a ruler. They need gardeners, parents, and mentors to empower and protect the seed of destiny.

**"When the Helper comes, whom I will send to you from the Father, that is the Spirit of truth who proceeds from the Father, He will testify about Me. . . . He will guide you into all the truth. . . . He will pour the love of God into your hearts"** (John 14:16; 16:13; Rom. 5:5).

## THE IMPORTANCE OF A SEED

Just like a seed in the natural, the Word of God within us will face the challenge of: breaking out of containment, believing against odds, pushing past comforts, standing strong in adversity, and remaining true to its divine course. Our co-labor together with the Father, Son, and Holy Spirit is vital for the maturing of what God desires in our life, and in the earth.

God's Word within us is yearning to grow—it has a journey to make, a course to finish, a destiny to fulfill . . . but it needs a favorable environment—a heart that is yielded to Him.

For too long the enemy has had his "hay-day" of stealing valuable fruit and destiny from the people of God—withering and choking the life out of them, out of us . . . stealing a harvest meant to glorify God and release His Kingdom on earth.

But no more.

Jesus, the Last Adam, has given us life and power to be a fruitful harvest of God's children who bring healing to the nations. All creation is waiting for the redeemed ones to release it from the corruption imposed on it from *our* fall. The earth is groaning, longing for the release of the anointing within you and me and our identity in Christ.

**"Creation waits in eager expectation for the sons of God to be revealed"** (Rom. 8:19 NIV).

In the following chapters, we will look at the different soil environments, both favorable and unfavorable, for growing seed . . . soil that is described by the most successful Man and Gardener on earth—Jesus Christ.

# 4

# THE SEED SNATCHER

*"When anyone hears the word of the kingdom
and does not understand it, the evil one comes
and snatches away what has been sown in his heart.
This is the one on whom seed was sown beside the road."*
—*Jesus (Matthew 13:19)*

The first type of soil that Jesus mentioned was the ground *beside the path.* Now the "path" itself does not refer to a trail for traffic, but the special course prepared by the gardener where he will plant his precious crop. Here the seed is nestled into the soil beneath a comforting blanket of rich earth. *"Beside the path"* is where foot traffic occurs, where the ground is hard and unprepared, so the seed just lays there—exposed to the fowl hovering above who are just waiting to gobble a tasty morsel of grain. A gobbled grain is a gobbled harvest.

Likewise, when the word that God speaks to us is not *planted* in a prepared heart, whether because we didn't understand it, didn't really grasp it, or were deceived into believing something else, it leaves the word vulnerable to the snatching schemes of demonic fowl. The word that is snatched means no fruit, no harvest.

The key element here in this first type of soil that we are going to look at, is a veiled understanding produced by *deception*. Deception is defined as the art of leading someone to believe something that is not true in order to gain some personal advantage. Have you ever been deceived? Of course you have. We all have at some time or another. And the feeling we experience when we learn the truth is one of feeling betrayed, duped, conned . . . stolen from.

The following story is based on a true event about deception and the most valuable seed ever snatched away—the seed of God's Word.

## THE SEED AND THE SERPENT

Eve lay on the moss that cushioned her body like a soft green pillow. Her hand gently stroked the lion resting beside her. She loved this beautiful garden that was home to her and Adam. It was rich with fruit trees, plants of every kind, and unique animals that Creator God had designed from His limitless imagination. Giggling at the anteater that was tickling her face and running his wet nose over her slender neck, she reached up to pat his head.

A gentle breeze brushed over her soft skin as she lay beneath the warm afternoon sun. Gazing into the deep blue of the afternoon sky she pondered Father's words, *"Be fruitful, multiply, and have dominion."*

"Have dominion." Hmm, Eve had no model for what dominion should look like; no books on leadership, no manuals of war, no history to learn from about governing a territory. What she did have was a word from God and His daily counsel. He said that she and Adam were to satisfy themselves from all the trees of the garden, except one: they were not to eat of the tree of the knowledge of good and evil for it would cause death. What is "death"? she wondered.

Lost in thought, she was unaware of the serpent that had come into the garden and was now just a foot away. The presence of darkness came seeking the daughter of light.

He spoke. She listened.

"Did God really say you would die if you ate from that tree?" the creature questioned.

"Oh, we aren't even supposed to touch it!" she replied.

"He's a liar!" bellowed the serpent with a hiss. "He's hiding something from you. He didn't give you the real picture, the true story. He's holding out on you. Don't be so naïve. Look. Take a good look at it! It will make you wise. As wise as God Himself! . . . and He doesn't want that."

Her mind was stunned with such words, such accusations against the Creator, yet something else was transpiring, too. Something was happening inside her heart that was being caressed with a luring promise. She rose and stood, taking in the words that brought reproach upon her Father, yet words that were stirring a strange new desire within her.

Could it be so? Could this creature know more about Creator than she? Was she . . . was Adam . . . were they mistaken regarding what God said? Had they been deceived by Father? She glanced upward, then toward the forbidden tree to which the creature was now pointing. Her eyebrows furrowed. She contemplated the Father's command. She considered the creature's poignant invitation.

Eve stood at the crossroad of deception. Two paths. A place to veer. She had never heard a lie or even a half-truth. She was perplexed, confused. She felt overwhelmed—a feeling she'd never known before. Yet at the same time a new discovery, a gold mine, that could be all hers!

A veil clouded her mind. Her spiritual eyes dimmed as her soul filled with a dark mist. She had no concept of life apart from God, no knowledge of the realms of evil that awaited her should she agree with the voice that was void of light. She had no idea as to the valuable treasure she held in having God's Word, or that she was about to trade it for fool's gold.

**"The commandment of the Lord is pure [unmixed], enlightening the eyes"**—David  (Ps. 19:8 clarification mine).

Father's words that had lain on the surface of her thoughts were now obscured by doubt that shadowed His absolute goodness. Could she trust Him? Was He trustworthy? Or was there a greater treasure to be had?

**"Your word have I hidden within my heart, that I might not sin against You"** — David (Ps. 119:11 NKJV).

She and Adam were given authority over the earth. The commission was clear, the mandate simple. The tree looked very pleasant to the eyes as something to make one wise . . . just like God. She knew she needed wisdom. She wanted it. Here was a chance to have it. All on her own. She could be all grown up, independent, leave home to "find herself". Certainly it could only produce something good in her life. Surely God was mistaken about this good-looking tree.

So there she was, juice dripping from her lips, standing naked, holding a fool's gold of knowledge in her hand. Meanwhile, the thief snuck away with her royal cloak and crown, leaving her with only chains to adorn her.

**"There is a way which seems right to a man, but its end is the way of death"** (Prov. 16:25).

## THE BATTLE FOR DOMINION

*Righteous dominion* excels when the one in authority *discerns* the intentions and presence of darkness, stops its advance, and casts it out.

*Bondage* ensues when the one in authority partners with darkness.

In the garden, the voice of authority fell silent. The voice of the light-bearer was muted as deceptive shadows coiled their web around her mind, plucking the seed of God's Word from her heart. The deceiver's trap of distraction and unbelief was a success—the word would not be fruitful in her life.

Why was she silent? Because in that moment—like moments we all have—the luring words that *seemed* so true, and the appeal to meet her need in her own way, rang louder than the still small voice within. A lure we are all too familiar with . . . a keenly devised strategy from a scheming adversary in a war for the Father's harvest.

God's command had been given to Eve, not to control her, but to *empower* and mature her as a righteous ruler—a radiant warrior, defender of the homeland, overcomer of the evil one, and mother of such lineage. God's Word and commands are NEVER about control, but about empowerment. But God's Word, unplanted and unbelieved, was unprotected; it lay vulnerable to the circling of hell's birds of prey as the deceivingly beautiful father of lies now stood before her, sowing his enticing words into her mind.

And she ate them.

She swallowed them—hook, line, and sinker. And that devilishly deceptive line yanked her out of the realm of glory and from her place of authority, plunging her into the dark realm of bondage.

Darkness reigns when Abba's children allow the devil into their garden, and agree with him.

## A WORLD OF WORDS

No one wants to feel like they've been deceived, but we've all been there. So how can we discern truth? How can we know the sound of a lie from the echo of God's truth, *and* the clear intention of both? How can our heart not be swayed toward evil? For certainly, no matter how delicious demonic words seem, they lead our soul to the pit of destruction. But God's Words, no matter how *seemingly* simple, lead our soul to glory realms of indescribable light and empowerment.

**We experience His glory every time we listen and do what Father God says.**

We live in a world of words. The earth itself was created by words—the Creator's words, **"Let there be . . . "** Mankind was formed in the image of the speaking God to be a people of divine words, a race of truth communicators. It was a perfect world, a safe world . . . until another voice, with other words, came along saying, "Has God *really* said?"

That doubt-casting voice created a different world: a fallen world where the heart awakens to a vision that is not from the Creator, but from a self-centered image with a deceptive beauty that kills the spirit and imprisons the soul.

What was once a simple life for Eve now became complicated, a world convoluted with differing voices. Far differing voices. The voice of truth and the voice of lies—lies whirling to distract her from her labor in the garden for Father's purposes.

Life is like that, isn't it? We find ourselves surrounded, bombarded, engulfed in a sea of sound from many sources with messages that beckon our attention, thoughts that demand our decisions, both conscious and unconscious. We get distracted, off track, way-sided from what is really important, from our original call . . . from the voice of God.

What is the truth? What is the lie? People say it's *this*, our flesh says it's *that*, and our societal culture has a "truth" all its own.

**"Your Word is truth"** — Jesus (John 17:17b).

Like a garden that grows whatever seed is planted there, so our life develops according to the seed of thought that resounds within us and takes root. Where do our thoughts take us? Toward God or away from Him?

The world speaks. The devil speaks. Our flesh speaks. Circumstances speak. But more importantly, God speaks. He whispers His heart and purpose to us day and night.

"But I can't hear God!" we cry. Are we listening? Are we seeking to hear? Some are, but perhaps our challenge is in understanding *what* He is saying or *how* is speaking to us (we will look more at how to hear God in chapter seven). Or perhaps God's words are being veiled by the deceiver's schemes so he can snatch them away from our heart's garden. Or maybe we are treating what God has said too lightly. I know I have on too many counts, but I'm learning to treasure them, so they become fruitful in my life, not stolen away.

## THE VOICE OF GOD

We are surrounded by a creation that declares the presence of God: the heavens declare His glory, constellations reveal His story, and every part of earth confesses to a Sovereign Designer. God's talking resonates with His love; it echoes a Fatherly involvement. We dream and He enters our scenes with divine dialogue to impart some truth to our spirit-man. We wake and we hear Him speak through a thought, a picture, a feeling, a song. We go about our day and He ministers to us through a word in Scripture, a song in the heart, an "aha" moment in a movie, a co-worker's encouragement, a friend's timely phone call . . . the list is endless. God is not limited in how He communicates with me, with you, with anyone.

He speaks with kings and the lowliest of men. Scripture itself is written by the inspiration of the Holy Spirit through the pen of shepherds, fishermen, murderers, prophets, kings, warriors, judges, pastors, doctors . . . who all heard the voice of God.

God wants to teach us to discern His voice from another, to hear His voice over the muddle of sound that surrounds us. Until we, like sheep amidst a world of thieves, hear the Good Shepherd and follow Him. Only Him.

**"My sheep hear My voice, and I know them, and they follow Me"** — Jesus (John 10:27).

What is the voice most clear in your head? In your heart? In your spirit? Recognize it! Your destiny depends on it. **"For as he thinks in his heart, so is he"** (Prov. 23:7a).

## THE POWER OF WORDS

Have you ever noticed how certain people stir certain aspects of your personality or nature, whether it's spiritual hunger, a side of humor, an irritable attitude, or desire to do mischief? Just their presence elicits an inward response. Like a giant tuning fork vibrating at a particular frequency, their nearness awakens a resonation within you.

Such is the power of personal influence and the kind of spirit a person carries. That's why it's important to be careful with who we allow to personally influence us. The devil is a liar and exaggerator, and you can see his influence already at work in Eve when she said, *"No, we aren't even supposed to touch it!"* But that wasn't what God said. He said they were not to *eat it.* God said nothing about *touching* it. And when Satan said that her words weren't true, he was right! Snap went the trap. Now off balance, her mind spun off course. One of Satan's favorite "tuning forks" is exaggeration that leads to suspicion, moving our mind to resonate with negative drama and creating the illusion of a *bigger, better, or worse than ever* appearance to things. She exaggerated what God said and she saw the tree *better* than it was.

Satan always makes sin look better and God meaner.

The devil is not a creator, but a conjuror. He loves to conjure up false perceptions to make us ponder, and in pondering his lies, they become our reality—a false certainty that misshapes our perspectives and motivates our decisions toward *his* goals. That's what happened to Eve. It's what happens to us every time we look at temptation, pick up an offense, or make preconceived judgments against others, against God, against ourselves.

Can you think of a personal circumstance in which your thoughts may have been a bit exaggerated? Just a bit?

Maybe we can question whether Eve really understood what God said. After all, she was still hidden within Adam's form when God gave them the command (not yet having been taken from his side). No doubt they talked about it later over dinner . . . she knew. But what did she *understand*? A mere "do and don't," a good rule of thumb, a proper principle to live by?

What do we understand when God speaks to us? Is it more like just a good idea? Again, **God speaks to empower life.**

**"He who has ears to hear, let him hear"**—Jesus (Matt. 11:15).

God's Word was given to Eve as a seed to cultivate and keep— that was part of her "dominion" training that would shape her as a child who sought not her own will, but Father's. She was a daughter in the school of the Spirit being educated for the purposes of God in the earth, for her generation . . . and those that would follow. Just as every child of God is in His training school. Watchman Nee said, *"Without submission there is no authority."* Submitting to God and resisting the devil was part of her training in authority.

The seed snatcher came to divert more than just her attention, and steal more than just her affection. He came to take her dominion over the earth and leave her a slave to her own wayward desires. Hmm, so familiar . . . his schemes never change.

## THE ART OF DISTRACTION

Beguilement. We've all experienced it—gazing on something that captures our attention and then leads us, like ignorant fools, into error and compromise; but it dazzles us with the promise of something desirable, irresistible. We are swayed by lightless words, influenced by a fallen creation.

Deceiving spirits watch with intent to snatch our potential, to get us off-track, and divert us from destiny by enticing us onto the wayside. No wonder Jesus is called the *Way*. He is the good ground where God's Word is heard and understood. Jesus said, *"Abide in Me."* In other words, don't get sidetracked because outside of Christ are other voices that will lead you astray!

**"Abide [remain] in Me, and I in you. As the branch cannot bear fruit of itself unless it abides in the vine, so neither can you unless you abide in Me"**—Jesus (John 15:4, clarification mine).

God wants us to listen to Him. He says that He speaks to us by the Son: **"God, who at various times and in various ways spoke in time past to the fathers by the prophets, has in these last days** spoken to us by His Son, whom He has appointed heir of all things, through whom also He made the worlds." (Heb.1:1-2). Why do you think there is so much attack on the name of Jesus? It is an attack on you and me being able to hear the voice of God in His Son, and thus be fruitful children.

No one can steal our destiny unless we let them, but we have an enemy who sure tries. We live in a world that does not believe God and that treats His Word lightly, without the honor He deserves. It so often influences us to do the same. The enemy of our soul is skilled in the art of stealing the Word of God from our heart through:

- **Distraction** so that God's voice is ignored
- **Deception** so that God's voice is mistrusted
- **Disobedience** so that God's voice is disregarded

Eve was side-tracked and died, falling short of divine destiny as the governess of the earth. That serpent the devil (the deceptive seed snatcher) and his sniveling servants did not somehow vanish from planet earth that day of man's fall. No! They are still at work to disengage the children of men from the voice of God lest they become fruitful, multiply, and have dominion on the earth.

The seed snatcher wants his darkness to rule our life, family, community, and nation. He wants our prayer life and intimacy with God to be a barren wasteland. He wants the seed of God's Word to be unfruitful in us, unsuccessful through veiled understanding—through a heart that is side-tracked.

How receptive is the soil of your heart to the Word of God? How trustworthy do you feel His Word is?

What are you listening to? Where is the enemy trying to get you off course? What is the distraction? Many voices call our attention: circumstances, fears, lusts of our flesh, people's opinions, failures, worldly philosophy, wounds of the heart, grudges, self-centeredness, complacency, busyness—we know them well . . . voices that snatch away our harvest.

What seed is the enemy trying to keep from being fruitful in your life?

What . . .

- **Divine revelation** is going unnoticed?
- **Spiritual gift** is being unused?
- **Kingdom talent** is being undeveloped?
- **Dream from God** is being dismissed as "just a thought"?
- **Anointed artistry, inventions, and business ideas** are not being brought from heaven to earth through earthly hands whose heart is in heaven, left in the unseen because of sidetracking, because of not understanding them as the voice of God?

Do you remember the last word God spoke to you? Think about it. How are you engaging it? Do you understand it? Or have you dismissed His speech merely as a "sound like thunder," just an idea, a fleeting impression, a passing feeling? What has He spoken to you through His Word? When was the last time you read His Word? What are you doing with what He said? What kind of soil environment are you giving God's voice in your life?

Take some time to review what He has said to you. Then write down:

**What God spoke to me:** _____

**How I am engaging it:** _____

**"It is the glory of kings to search out a matter"** (Prov. 25:2b).

The seed of God's Word is a treasure waiting to be hid in the heart that will receive it. It is looking for a heart that understands it with their spirit, not merely by their mind. The earth is also waiting, longing for the sons and daughters of God to return to dominion as the healing governors of this planet. The seed snatchers are waiting, too, for divine and prophetic words that we ignore and mistrust, hovering with desire to whisk them away to the camp of Unfulfilled Destiny.

**The heart that receives and believes what God says will surely find its way to fulfilled destiny.**

*Father, forgive me for not receiving Your words and promises to me. Forgive me for listening to so many other voices, for getting distracted instead of engaging with Your voice. I reclaim the seed that the enemy has stolen and I plant it in my heart now. Help me, Holy Spirit, to treasure it above all things so that it grows, unhindered, into fruitfulness in my life—fruit that glorifies You. I love You, Father. In Jesus' name, Amen.*

# 5

## THE FATE OF THE WITHERED SEEDLING

*"The one on whom seed was sown in the rocky places, this is the man who hears the word and immediately receives it with joy; yet he has no firm root in himself, but is only temporary, and when affliction or persecution arises because of the word, immediately he falls away."*
—*Jesus (Matt. 13:20-21)*

The second type of soil that the Most Successful Man talked about was the rocky soil. In a way, you could say that this kind of soil carries "extra baggage"—places in the heart that have hardened whether through pride or pain, or both. These cause us to respond poorly in times of adversity—"poorly" meaning that the flourishing of God's Word in us has found a stopping point.

Rocks—hardness in the heart, strongholds of the soul—prevent our roots from going deep in God, thwarting the advancement of growth, and thus a withering in times of adversity.

As we look at the plight of a seed in rocky soil, we begin with a true story of a man whose faith withered in the heat of adversity.

### THE MAN WITH LITTLE ROOTS

Adam stood there, dumbfounded. His chest throbbing. Eve's

71

hand reached out to him in loving gesture, inviting him to join her wayward intrigue. His mind raced. Soon Father would be there for His usual afternoon visit. And there stood Eve, doing just what Father said not to do . . . eating from the forbidden tree.

Father's instruction raced through his brain. His stomach churned. His world was torn.

"Oh God, what do I do?"

He pictured the moment that Father had told him, "Of all the trees of the garden you may freely eat, but not of the tree of the knowledge of good and evil. For in the day you eat of that tree, you will surely die." He remembered the deep love he felt for Father; scenes played on the screen of his imagination of how he would nobly uphold Dad's command and defend His name, like a true son.

Now the moment of testing had come. He felt the sword of loyalty slipping from his hand. He could tell that Eve was seeing things that he did not see, experiencing things of which he was ignorant. Was this what it meant to "die"? But she seemed, happy.

They were in two different worlds. How could he live without her? The choice was grueling: Father or his wife. His wife was part of him—bone of his bone, flesh of his flesh. How could he deny his own flesh?

Her voice echoed with sweet desire, "Come with me."

This was not part of the plan!

The cost of losing her gripped him. He could not bear the thought of life without Eve. After all, the Creator Himself had said it was not good for Adam to be alone! So Adam reached toward Eve . . . surely Father would understand.

**"Casting down every imagination that raises itself against the knowledge of God"** —Paul (2 Cor. 10:5 WEB).

## THE HEAT OF ADVERSITY

Adam found himself in the midst of a conflict. The two who were one were now separated by an eternal gulf. But where was he when his wife fell into deception? Where was he when the devil entered the garden? Was he busy? Or was he standing nearby, curious as to what would happen? We don't know. We can't assume. We can't blame . . . like Adam did with Eve when Father came. Whatever Adam's reason, the bottom line is that his own lack of being rooted in the love of God was evident.

It is said that when the mind is tested, the condition of the heart is revealed.

We have all experienced adversity—unfavorable events, hardships, and sufferings in our life—that has tested what God has spoken to us. Adversity comes in myriad forms . . . and often expressly because of the identity we carry as God's children. Remember, we have an enemy seeking our harvest.

All through Scripture, men and women of God were tested regarding God's plan for them. For Abraham, it was the long wait for a promised heir . . . and then the word to slay him. For Moses, it was decades of hiding in the desert before his calling came to fruition. For Joseph, it was a long wait to be released from an unjust prison house and for the sovereign fulfillment of a God-given dream. For David, it was years of running for his life until the crown sat on his head. And for young Daniel, it was a hostile exile from his beloved homeland and relocation as a servant to a pagan nation.

In our own life, we've heard God speak, we have felt His presence, we've received His guidance. We knew it was God; it brought change to our life. Then comes the difficulty because of the word: a friend forsakes us, a loved one betrays us, finances fail us. Confrontations arise as associations, activities, and involvements change. We are faced with difficult choices. We are ignored, overlooked, people don't affirm us, an illness takes hold of us and robs our strength. Our dreams are shelved, maybe we feel like they've died. We feel confused, and we don't like it. But there it is. We feel like we are standing alone, under pressure, against all odds, in the face of rejection.

There are times when we feel the heat of what is at stake if we continue believing the word we know was from God—the direction He gave, or perhaps the promise He spoke. We dig deep into our pocket to see if we have enough to pay the cost of doing the right thing. Sometimes we have what it takes, but other times we know we've come up short.

Life's challenges can be like a searing sun withering a young plant that has not found a deep root system. We want to be mighty trees of valor, but in moments of temptation our weakness sometimes wins. It's easy to grow in pleasant circumstances, but a plant's growth isn't just an upward journey into the beautiful sunshine, but a *downward extension* as well—sending roots deep to draw from hidden streams. That is where the life source exists from which a plant draws true strength.

**Life is lived *from* the unseen toward the seen—from the *inside* out.**

Job—the man most noted for being tested through adversity—said that the branches of the *wicked* are cut off because their roots have dried up. They live in a waterless place. They may be prosperous for a season, but eternal destinies are defined by root systems.

In Francis Frangipane's book, *The Three Battlegrounds* (Revised edition), he writes:

*"We will never know Christ's victory in its fullness until we stop reacting humanly to our circumstances. . . .Satan's arsenal consists of such things as fear, worry, doubt and self-pity. Every one of these weapons robs us of peace and leaves us troubled inside."*

The author also goes on to explain how the battles we go through can become experiences that nourish and build us up, as we discern life's challenges through being deeply rooted in God's love.

It isn't easy to ignore the difficult situations we face everyday, the time delay, the failed expectation, the hurtful losses. Sometimes it's easier to discount what God says, throw in the towel, find something else to do. Or like Peter—return to what you knew before when all seems lost.

"Another time perhaps, God. . . . This is impossible! . . . I can't do this. . . . I need them. . . . I need that. . . . I'll lose everything. . . .

I don't know how to do this. . . . I see no way through. . . . It'll never happen."

You know the thoughts that come.

**"By faith, Abel—Enoch—Noah—Abraham—Sarah—Isaac— Jacob—Rahab—Gideon—men and women of old . . . gained approval"** (Heb. 11). These understood that faith without *action* is an incomplete faith experience (James 2:22).

These people, like David, walked a moment in the *shadow of death*, but were not overcome with fear. God's presence was the anchor of their soul. His peace was their victory. They were convinced that it was impossible for God to lie; they were persuaded regarding the unchangeableness of His character and the kind intentions of His heart toward them. Like Paul, the roots of their heart went deep into a confidence in God that He alone was the greatest Prize of all, and that He was with them. Thus, they were not alarmed by their adversity.

**"Blessed is the man who perseveres under trial"** (James 1:12).

God has a way of building "spiritual muscle" in us through adversity. Father wants us strong—not blown about by every wind or wincing like whiners. Recently, I was working out at the gym with my personal trainer who is helping me to get fit. He *always* pushes me beyond my comfort zone, and if he sees I'm doing "well" he will increase the intensity. However, if he sees me really struggling, he will help *lift* the weight, but he won't *remove* the weight or stop the training session. One day, he brought me to a piece of equipment to work on strengthening my "core". He commented that ninety percent of the people he sees using that machine, use it improperly.

"Doing so," he said, "they end up riding a momentum, but not building muscle."

God knows how to build us up in our identity in Him, even in the midst of adversity. He builds our spiritual fiber through the storms we encounter and difficulties that challenge us. He wants more than our "riding a momentum," He wants us "fit" for the position we carry as His children, as earth rulers with Him.

## DEATH IN THE SHALLOWS

**"They will be called oaks of righteousness, a planting of the Lord for the display of His splendor"**—Isaiah (Isa. 61:3 NIV).

God says that His children are the planting of His hand—Oak trees to be specific. Oak trees require deep soil where roots can grow and firmly anchor themselves. They seek deep, moist places *beyond the shallows*. Other kinds of trees have shallow root systems. But not Oaks.

**"Deep calls to deep"**—David (Ps. 42:7).

God says that the *leaves* (expressed growth) of His children are for the healing of the nations. The nations need healing. Nations are people, communities, cultures, and governments. Look around you. Read the paper. Watch the news (if you can stand it). People are desperate for the touch of God. People's hearts that don't know the life-giving waters of God are dry. Scorched. They look for water at surface levels. Surface levels carry a lot of toxins. But people are desperate—they'll get water from any place they can, any stream will do.

Let's re-visit our earlier story: Eve was now in bondage and spiritually dead—a waterless place. Adam was about to enter the same. Sometimes, when the heart is drawn away, it's easier to join the one in darkness than to try and throw them a life-line. I mean, really. Adam had a choice. He knew what he was doing. He wasn't "deceived". Eve didn't force him to eat the fruit of sin. What would have happened had Adam asked Father God for wisdom in that situation? What solution did the Divine have for him in that difficult moment? Certainly God had an answer. He always does. What if Adam had stood firm and asked the Creator to somehow save her—instead of disobeying the Father to willingly join her folly . . . and then blaming her for his own choice?

We all have our "what ifs," but we can't look back except to learn. We only have this moment. What is His answer for us, for our situation, in *this* moment?

The shallow is where the *natural mind* lives. It takes into account only what the natural eye sees, and what one's own ability provides. It lives in a narrow, limited place. It sees the moment, but doesn't *seize* the moment with the display of God's glory in mind. It thinks of itself.

In the shallow places, a seedling has to vie for space and contend for life by squeezing itself between rocks and stones where it can then comfortably bask beneath the warm sun . . . but not *too* warm, not the blazing sun. Rocks and stones represent hard places embedded in the heart—mindsets that are stubborn, unbendable, unteachable, and unyielding. These patterns of thought abort a fruitful destiny for a seed that requires tender soil to go deep.

The natural mind loves the message of the blessing that the

Kingdom brings. As long as everything is convenient, we thrive. We prosper on the surface water of people's affirmation, financial success, and good health. Zippity doo dah! . . . Wonderful feeling, wonderful day! Surely God is with us. He is blessing us! We have a great job, great spouse, our kids behave and our hair looks nice. We have this Christianity thing down pat. Just ask me the question and I'll spit out the right Scripture. By golly, I'm God's favored . . . no—favorite!

But then, out comes the blazing sun of adversity, searing and burning our flesh. What then? Do our roots hit rocks of offense? Stones of pride? Boulders of bitterness? What is our attitude? Are we offended with God? Do we rage at people? Or maybe just sizzle silently in a stew? Do we seek for God to reveal *His* way, or do we demand our own? Do we lift a hand of praise or a fist of anger? Especially, if the sun has blazed with record heat for an intolerable number of days. Do we choose a path that is contrary to what God has said?

## WATER—A MOST ESSENTIAL ELEMENT FOR LIFE

Standing firm is the result up **water uptake**. In plant life, we call it *turgidity*—water drawn into the cells that enable the plant to stand upright. Water is a MOST ESSENTIAL element to all forms of life on planet Earth. Water provides the means by which plants obtain essential nutrients from the soil; the deprivation of it results in stunted growth. Water is fundamental for the success of a seed. A lack of water can mean a failed harvest.

It is no different for our spiritual life and the strength of our soul—we need the water of God's Word, His voice. We also need

His comfort. That's why we've been sent the Comforter—the Holy Spirit. "Comfort" means: with strength, with fortitude. **We need the constant current of the Holy Spirit's presence, truth, and comfort to grow us, help us stand under duress, comfort us in troubles, and encourage us when we are weak.** We need His revelation to give our inner man the needed power for our outer man's challenges. We need His understanding to be able to absorb the nutrients in Scripture so that we don't have merely head knowledge, but intimate heart knowledge that results in a transformed life.

We need intimate fellowship with Jesus whose voice *"is the sound of many waters"* to give us a renewed strength and grace beyond our own ability.

The Holy Spirit will comfort and strengthen us through prayer, meditation in God's Word, and by the encouraging touch of others. God's name is *"Fountain of Living Water"* for a reason; the water of His presence is a MOST ESSENTIAL element for life and godliness, and for the days in which we live.

King David understood this in his relationship with God and implored the Lord to never take away His Holy Spirit. David knew his source of power—that the watering presence of the Word and Spirit made him like a "green olive tree" in the house of God. Such presence captivated his heart with love, and instilled in him an unceasing trust in God's lovingkindness, no matter what (Ps. 52:8).

The drinking in of divine love and comfort creates a holy unwillingness to leave the Shepherd's side for another voice. The love of the Spirit inspires the heart with a trust in God that won't give up, that perseveres—such perseverance that is willing to embrace the cross, die to self, and lean on divine counsel instead of our own understanding. Perseverance requires engagement with the person of the Holy Spirit, rather than the mind of the flesh.

The thoughts of our heart need the mind of the Spirit.

**God isn't raising wimpy kids made of straw who blow away with every wind. He's raising rulers—governors that flourish with righteous dominion over powers of darkness.**

Unfortunately—for we who like a bed of roses—people don't always do what we want them to do, or act the way we want them to act. God doesn't always do what we want either, or when we want! His answers aren't always what we want to hear. I personally find His processes waaaay too long. As my mother so often said, "I want it done yesterday!"

Have you ever noticed how much we like to control life, God, and those around us?

## HARDNESS IN THE HEART

We can say that rocks and stones are the natural formation of the carnal mind where layers of **pride, self-will,** and **strongholds** run deep within our soul. The carnal mind is set on the flesh and is death to our spiritual identity. This mind with its fleshly boulders stands against the knowledge of God. These give us excuses for no longer believing God when times are tough, for falling away when misfortune visits, or when painful things happen that we can't understand. They obscure the memories of what God has already done in our life, of the joy we felt when we first believed—of when we first felt His love and heard Him speak to us. Such hardness blocks our ability to draw from Him as our source of life.

There we stand, once excited with a bright future, but now tempted to turn our back because of some unwanted tribulation on our doorstep. We feel like the rug has been yanked out from under us. Persecution's arrow has entered our back, and come clean through our heart.

Difficulties—endless, unexplainable, inexcusable, unjustifiable difficulties surround us, taunting our faith. Overwhelming challenges meet us at an unexpected turn. Heart breaking situations encounter us to devastate us.

What shall we do?

**"These things I have spoken to you, so that in Me you may have peace. In the world you have tribulation, but take courage; I have overcome the world"**—Jesus (John 16:33).

We don't like the thought of trouble, but God says that even the righteous pass through many afflictions, but that He delivers us out of them all (Ps. 34:19). Joshua, the great leader of Israel who led them into battle for their inheritance, was no stranger to troubles. Yet, he said, **"As for me and my house, we will serve the Lord"** (Josh. 24:15). Life has its troubles, but we are never out of Father's sight, His loving care, or divine provision. Even Jesus learned obedience through the things He suffered. . . . And He came out perfect!

My question is: what was lacking in Adam's heart that God was somehow not enough for him? What is the stronghold in my heart that hinders my own deep rooting in God? David, in the Old Testament, discovered that nothing in life compares to the presence

THE FATE OF THE WITHERED SEEDLING

of God: **"You are my Lord; apart from you I have no good thing"** (Ps. 16:2 NIV).

Fortunately, we get to learn on our journey. We can learn from our mistakes, and those of others, too. Adam's first big lesson was: self-centeredness kills! Thank God for grace that renews and delivers.

**"If anyone comes to Me, and does not hate his own father and mother and wife and children and brothers and sisters, yes, and even his own life, he cannot be My disciple"**—Jesus (Luke 14:26).

It's easy to get offended with God and people in the midst of adversity. And if we don't get God's perspective (instead of relying on our own), offenses can multiply. We pick up one, then another. And before we know it, we've got a whole bag of them slung over our shoulder that we're carrying around everywhere we go. And the stones, oh the stones of *unforgiveness* that lay everywhere, piling up in the shallow place, standing as a memorial to our woes.

Hardness in the heart keeps us from tapping into the grace of God, the love of God, and the truth of God that refreshes and nurtures the heart in difficult times. Hardness prevents the soul from anchoring its confidence into the waters of God's Word, name, character, and nature. **And without this anchor, we cannot do the will of God.**

**And what's more, offenses and unloving actions are like murder. And, as with Cain, they will actually cause our ground to curse us, and no longer produce for us** (Gen. 4). This is why forgiveness is critical to a fruitful life; it makes the soil of our heart tender, and releases the ground to bless us in return.

## STRENGTHENING YOURSELF IN THE LORD

Life is full of twists and turns and painful events. Every single one of us can be tempted to throw in the towel and say: *How could they do that to me? Things will never change! Things didn't turn out the way I thought. I'm going back. I'm going to get even!* Self-soothing in self-pity is so easy.

We all feel like that sometimes, but what do we *do* with what we feel?

I remember one time I got angry over a promise made to me that was broken by someone I highly respected. It wasn't the first promise or word they had failed to follow through with, but this one was different. It was something deeply important to me. As my temperature gauge escalated, I felt the Holy Spirit tell me to not react in emotion. I went to bed and tossed and turned until the wee hours of the morning. Then I did it. I gave in to my flesh. I got up, opened my computer, and wrote an e-mail. I expressed just how I felt, but my words lacked grace. They were truth without love. I knew I was wrong, but continued anyway. And then I pressed "send".

I repented, but lamented over that action for months because it was not sent with the heart of God; it was sent with the stench of flesh being offended. As my mother used to say, "Two wrongs do not make a right."

King David was well acquainted with his own potential of moving on his emotions—of choices made contrary to the heart of God. He encouraged himself to keep his focus where it needed to be by talking to himself, saying things like, **"My soul, wait thou only on God; for my expectation is from Him"** (Ps. 62:5 WEB). He knew what to expect from his own flesh . . . deadly consequences from shallow thinking! David may have first ranted a while about his woes—not stuffing them or denying how he felt, but getting it out there, addressing his situation and emotions. But he tried to work it out in the presence of God because he knew how unruly flesh will kick the cat, sue the neighbor, and carry a club to the house of the offender. So David practiced sharing his sorrows with God, then asking Him to cleanse him from any state of heart that wasn't congruent with His truth and love. That didn't mean, however, that he didn't deal with unjust issues appropriately.

David admitted how he felt, but he chose not to stay there. He didn't want to remain in gloom and despair. That wasn't who he was! He was a son of God and he knew it. He got things off his chest with God and then spent time with the Holy Spirit tossing out—from his heart—the rocks of unbelief and stones of offense. He threw them, not at people, but into ponds . . . into the ponderings of God's ability. He strengthened his soul with the truth of God's faithful character. He spoke it, wrote it, sang it, danced it, prayed it, declared it—renewing his mind in the truth of God as a faithful Father, a caring Teacher, and a Mighty Warrior who wars on behalf of those who love Him.

**"David strengthened himself in the Lord"** (1 Sam. 30:6). He drew comfort from God, not from a bottle of rum or people's affirmation. David had a destiny to fulfill. A destiny with God. Not with his flesh or with the world, but with God.

David was an Old Testament guy with a New Covenant theology. He knew that the Kingdom of God and its power is found beyond the shallows—beyond where flesh meets with circumstances—but where the heart meets with God.

Adam wasn't meeting with God when he made his choice in the shallows. How many choices have you and I made without meeting with God first?

## REMOVING THE STONES

Thank God that seed growing is a JOURNEY! We learn as we grow. God wants us to believe that He is bigger than the problem, the difficulty, or the tribulation. He wants our victory more than we do! But He also knows that victory isn't always about what happens to us, but what is happening *in* us. He wants us to understand that He has answers that we may not yet see.

If we've fallen in the face of difficulty, He says, **"A righteous man falls [fails] seven times and rises again"** (Prov. 24:16a, clarification mine). We get up! We grab the Hand of God who pulls us to our feet. We brush off the dust and take a giant swig of grace to quench our parched throat . . . parched from all the complaining and whining. But the wicked, He says, stagger in calamity; they fall and do not rise in faith. We, however, are not of those who draw back and perish, but of those who believe to the saving of the soul.

As gardeners, we must till our soil and remove the stones and rocks. Why?

1. Because we have vision for a *full* harvest; we want our seed to be successful

2. Because there ARE hard places inside us! Places stubborn to the Spirit

Now here's an interesting fact I learned recently from a friend who lives on a farm: in days gone by, a garden tractor that was used to dig deep into the earth to remove unwanted stones before planting a crop was called a **"repentance plow"**.

Jesus came preaching, **"Repent for the Kingdom of heaven is at hand"** (Matt. 4:17). There is nothing harder than the human heart that is apart from the love of God. And there is nothing that tenderizes the heart so much as true repentance—not being "sorry," lamenting you got caught, or apologizing out of self-embarrassment, but embracing the conviction of the Holy Spirit and turning toward God for lasting change. Repentance is the first step of creating a nurturing environment to the Word of God in our life. It is the first step of obedience we take in following the Son as we return to Father.

**"Break up your fallow ground, and do not sow among thorns"** (Jer. 4:3b).

Repentance prepares the heart for deep, effective growth of God's Word inside us. Repentance *empowers* the seedling of our identity in Christ to rise triumphant in the midst of tribulation, adversity, and persecution. We not only come through, but we come out stronger, and more in the likeness of the Son who is God's manifest love.

**"Love . . . is not arrogant . . . it does not seek its own, is not provoked, does not take into account a wrong suffered . . . bears all things, believes all things, hopes all things, endures all things. . . . If you love Me, you will keep My commandments"** (I Cor. 13; John 14:15).

## THE PRACTICE OF GOD'S PRESENCE

Every tribulation is an opportunity to discover God in new ways, and in new depth. As we allow His Kingdom to take more ground inside us, it can then more easily be released through us.

We can either live in the shallows where the scorching heat of adversity withers us—where people have hurt us, rejected us, where pride drives us, where disappointments wound us—or we can repent, turn to God, and drink of His presence. We can ask our Heavenly Gardener to break the hardness of our heart, root-out self, remove offense, and send our roots deep into the waters of His love . . . love that *bears all things, weathers storms, and stands firm in the midst of persecution.*

We *can* be like Abraham, that friend of God of whom it is said: **"yet, with respect to the promise of God, Abraham did not waver in unbelief but grew strong in faith, giving glory to God"** (Rom. 4:20). In this world we *will* have tribulation, and every word that God gives us *will* be tested. Will we be God's friend in those times? Even if He *seems* distant (but is not)?

In Brother Lawrence's classic book, *The Practice of the Presence of God,* he shares how a heart prepared for times of tribulation is one that practices the presence of God. It is continually searching deep into His Word and drinking from the living water table of His presence that flows in the place beyond the shallows. Honestly, I don't know if anyone is ever *fully* prepared for unexpected tribulation, as it is something we meet in the moment—something we must meet in the moment *with God.* In my life, I have known times when I have soared with strong wings in adverse winds. I have also known moments when I have struggled to keep afloat amidst overwhelming waves. But it wasn't for long, for there is a buoyancy of the Holy Spirit within the spirit of every true believer. And the one anchor and buoy that I have always found to steady me is, as Brother Lawrence found, the presence and love of God.

**"Watch over your heart with all diligence, for from it flows the springs of life . . ."**—Solomon (Prov. 4:23).

Adam's joy in walking with God withered when the Word of God was tested through tribulation. Its roots hit a hard place in Adam's heart. The result: a broken covenant and broken fellowship between a Father and son . . . and a son's unfulfilled destiny. It is the *condition of the heart* (not the condition of the circumstance) that either speeds along the growth of God's seed in our life, or hinders its way.

Faithfulness has a price and a reward; faith*lessness* has a cost, too—one without a reward and with consequences. It carries a loss that is greater than we will want to bear. With reason, God's Word says, **"Have this attitude in yourselves which was also in Christ Jesus. . . being found in appearance as a man, He humbled Himself by becoming obedient to the point of death, even death on a cross"** (Phil. 2:5, 8).

Who knows what might have been, what God could have done with the situation had Adam remained true. What if he had stood in the gap for his wife, had asked God for her redemption? Who knows what God can do in our situation, if we would dare to remove hardness and dig beyond the shallows to know God in the midst of our circumstance?

The message of the Kingdom is a faith in what is *not seen*—a faith in God that peers past, gazes beyond, and looks for what doesn't meet the physical eye. It digs deeper for spiritual insight into the heart of God for *His* answer to an onslaught, dilemma, confused state, or adversity. It *waits* on God to hear from Him. The DNA of God inside us looks for the nurturing depth of continued encounter with God's presence. Only as the heart's expectations are firmly rooted in Christ, can the seedling of our identity in Him continue to mature and withstand the adverse heat of our day.

**"Trust in the Lord with all your heart and lean not on your own understanding. In all your ways acknowledge Him and He will direct your paths"** (Prov. 3:5,6 NKJV).

*Upward growth and outward branches are determined by inward depth.*

Take some time and ask the Holy Spirit to show you where some of those hard places may be causing you to wither, be stuck, and not advance in your growth in Him. Write them out.

**Stubborn Mindset:** _____

**Area of Unforgiveness:** _____

**Action I need to take:** _____

*Abba Father, forgive me where I have leaned on my own understanding — for looking only with natural eyes that see the trouble, but not with spiritual eyes that see the triumph, for seeing only death and not a resurrection by Your power. I want to be Your friend who doesn't stumble in difficult times, but trusts You. Remove every stone of unbelief, pride, and offense. I choose to forgive those who have been instruments of harm in my life and I entrust them into Your hands, as well as the outcome of every situation I face. I accept Your timing as perfect, better than my own. I love You, Father. I want Your presence in my life. In Jesus' name, Amen.*

# 6

## THE CASE OF THE STRANGLED SAPLING

*"And others are the ones on whom seed was sown among the thorns; these are the ones who have heard the word, but the worries of the world and the deceitfulness of wealth, and the desires for other things enter in and choke the word, and it becomes unfruitful."*
*—Jesus (Mark 4:18-19)*

One day, as I was praying, I felt the Lord say, "Let's go for a walk." It sounded exciting and I thought, *oh, a new adventure with God!* In my spirit, I saw Him take me by the hand and walk me into a garden, one full of beautiful flowers and winding paths. There were other people there, too; each one occupied with what He was showing them. It appeared that He was with them individually just as He was with me. I asked what they were doing and He told me not to be concerned about that, but to simply focus on what He would show me. And show me, He did. The "adventure" unfolded into a season of tending my garden—weeding out undesirable plants and uprooting strangling vines. I had a destiny to fulfill and could not do so with their presence.

As a good Gardener, God truly cares about the condition of our heart, about the weeds and thorns that steal our fruitfulness. A weed is defined as a "plant out of place to a particular environment." The love of the world is a plant out of place in the heart of a son or daughter of God.

**"Do not love not the world nor the things in the world. If anyone loves the world, the love of the Father is not in Him"** (1 John 2:15).

So far, we have looked at the first two types of soil in which God's Word fails to see full fruitfulness in a life. Now we come to the third—one that also hinders the harvest of the holy seed within us. This is the soil that grows thorns and thistles right together with the good seed. It is called: a *neglected* garden.

Before we begin our study of this particular garden, I want to share another story—one based on a true event from the life of Jesus.

## THE STRANGLING OF A YOUNG RULER

The young man said good-night to his friends and started the short distance toward home. The party had been pleasurable and profitable as well, having made an important business transaction during dinner with a new partner. This would make his future a bright one. But as the laughter of the crowd faded, a familiar feeling crept over him. A place deep within him echoed with emptiness.

Trained as the son of a nobleman to be a leader in his community, success was important, one that included a right standing with the Almighty. He enjoyed a religious life, but a hollow feeling inside his heart nagged at him. It was as if God was whispering to him, summoning him to a journey of higher purpose. But he didn't know what that looked like. The feeling had come so often…it was time for an answer. Everything else in life was falling in line for him, but this one thing that tugged his heart needed to be settled: What was the eternal state of his soul?

A thought entered his mind—*I'll ask the Rabbi. He will know what I'm to do!*

The next morning the young man rose early to go to the temple. Hopefully he would find the Rabbi there. If not, surely someone would know where He was. He could hardly wait! He was convinced that this Rabbi—the Man of God who was currently the talk of the town because of His miracles—would have the answer he sought; then peace would come again to his agitated soul. With that in mind, he put on his finest clothes and set out.

Seeing the Rabbi on the road, he ran to meet Him and knelt before Him. Head bowed, his heart pounded. "Good Teacher," the young man said, "what good thing should I do that I might obtain eternal life?"

The Rabbi looked compassionately on him and replied, "Why do you call Me good? There is only One who is good, and that is God. But if you wish to enter into life, keep the commandments."

Wanting certainty, lest he presume his own goodness, the young man looked up at Him and questioned, "Which ones?"

The Teacher reached down, and lifting him up said, "Do not commit murder or adultery, and do not steal or bear false witness. Honor your father and mother, and love your neighbor as yourself."

The young man thought deeply over his life, confident that he had done his best in these matters of conduct. Still feeling a sense of need that he couldn't quite put his finger on, he responded, "I have done all these things! What am I still lacking?"

The Master put His hand on the young shoulder, and looking deep into his searching eyes said, "If you wish to be perfect, go and sell all that you have and give to the poor, then you will have treasure in heaven—then come and follow Me."

The young man was stunned. The answer so unexpected. His countenance fell as he stared at the ground . . . he was speechless. Pictures of all he possessed flooded his mind—career, position, estate . . . *his* future! It wasn't the answer he thought he'd receive. Could he not have eternal life without such loss? He stood there pondering, questioning, grief pounding through his soul. How could he give up so much?

*What should I do?* He thought. *Surely this Rabbi is wise, but this couldn't be the only way!*

He raised his eyes to meet the Master's. No words were needed. It was understood. The price was too high. The young man turned his gaze to the way that led back to the familiar, and he left.

**"For where your treasure is, there your heart will be also"** —Jesus (Luke 12:34).

## MIXTURE IN THE HEART

Do you ever wonder what happened to that young man? Or what would have become of his life had he sold all and followed Jesus? What if he'd dared to believe in something greater than earth's treasures? Who knows? He might have been another Apostle Paul.

Or, the Lord might have given back to him every thing he'd laid on the altar. Certainly he would have encountered the true riches of eternal life that his spirit hungered for—wealth that earth's money can't buy, but one which the King of heaven and earth provides.

Good seed was blossoming in this young man's life, but so was the love of the world. Such weedy affections strangled the seed of divine destiny in him and choked out the life and call of God. Divine purpose was smothered by self-serving purposes that darkened his eyes from seeing truth.

Mixture. Double-mindedness. One foot in God and the other in the world. A desire for the eternal and a love for the spirit of the world. We're all familiar with it—lusts that proliferate in-between the flowers of church activities and good works. We make sure that faith adorns our walkway in public view, but hidden beneath the foliage, where nobody sees, we've got poppy plants that fill our senses with fantasies of secret lusts—from selfish ambition to unholy affairs to fear, worry, and envious greed.

**"For all that is in the world, the lust of the flesh, the lust of the eyes, and the pride of life, is not of the Father, but is of the world"** (1 John 2:16).

## GOOD SEED—BAD SEED

**"You shall not sow your field with two kinds of seed"** (Lev. 19:19).

After mankind's fall away from Perfect Love, life was experienced *outside* the garden of God's presence. There the earth grew thorns and thistles, making man's labor on earth difficult. At that critical moment of mankind's fall, Satan was not only given opportunity to seize the scepter as the "god" of this world, but unseen currents of demonic power were unleashed over the earth; flows that act as an under-tow that continually pushes and pulls the heart of mankind away from the Creator. These currents are like a spiritual gravitational force that pulls people down and keeps them earthbound, rather than living from an identity of being seated with Christ in heavenly places. They are "winds" that carry and scatter another kind of seed—ungodly seed of thorny dark thoughts, devouring desires, and evil actions.

This is the spirit of the world that carries the seed of Satan's words. Its growth is a counterfeit vine that strangles life rather than giving it—a thorny creation that chokes the very breath of our spiritual life—and most of the time, we don't even realize it. Why? Because it is the *spirit* of the world in which we live, work, and move. It whispers its death into the mindsets of our cultures, personal choices, and even our religious traditions. And the one denominator these all have in common, and why we embrace them so easily, so nonchalantly, is that they all *seem so natural*—they are the "norm". "Everybody does it!" we say.

The weeds that spring from the devil's words are not good neighbors. They do not play well with other seed. They seek control. That is their goal. They are, after all, the offspring of a cursed being. As gardeners of our heart our job is to be diligent, vigilant for the well-being of our harvest. We have been given governorship. And what enemy we do not exercise rule over, will rule over us . . . no matter how pleasing or innocent its flowers may first appear.

The Master of fruitfulness named three specific types of thorny weeds that strangle the seed of God's Word in us:

1. Cares of this world
2. Deceitfulness of riches
3. Pleasures (lusts) of this life

Worries, wealth's deceit, and worldly pleasure are like thorns and thistles—plants out of place in the garden of our heart as God's children. They ravage the habitat created for God's presence, disrupting the ecosystem of love through their warring dominance. These, said Jesus, will destroy the harvest if left to grow in our soil. Did you hear that? They will entwine the holy seed and obliterate our intended destiny of fruitfulness. Their picture reminds me of how Kudzu vines (seen along southern U.S. highways) drape themselves over miles of landscape, veiling the identity of beautiful forests, sucking the life out of the mighty trees they cloak like a shroud.

As I was meditating on the cares, riches, and pleasures Jesus spoke of, I wondered if there might be a link between them. Is there a connection between gardens where worry, wealth priorities, and worldliness proliferate? The answer that came is, yes. And it is the three-fold chord of fear, lies, and compromise. Like three evil friends who incite each other to fiendish endeavors, these are spirits that cloak and choke our identity as God's children.

Let's look at the following three people and their circumstances.

- Jane is worried about her family—she continually worries about her husband's career, potential personal health issues, and their children's needs. Confident authority is replaced by crushing anxiety. She doesn't feel like praying, and uses her favorite T.V. shows to distract her mind. Passion shuts down and gives way to spiritual passivity; faith is compromised by the voice of fear.

- Joe is a great business man. He has a talent for making money. But no matter how much he makes, it is never enough. There is always something more he needs, more he wants, another position to pursue. He works longer hours and compromises his love for God by neglecting intimacy with Him and His Word. Home and good relationships aren't as important anymore either. There just isn't time.

- Julie loves parties and fun. She came from a broken home and never really felt accepted and valued. She looks for affirmation in relationships with men, who seem to care more about what they can get from her than for her well-being. She loves her church but doesn't go very often, doesn't get involved, doesn't make friends there—she fears rejection because of her choices and doesn't feel like she fits in. She compromises godly values and wise choices in an attempt to meet her own need; its choking her spiritual life.

If each continues on their path of compromise with the current of this world, the intended harvest meant for Jane, Joe, and Julie's life will not come to fruition, just as what happened with the rich young ruler.

The word "compromise" means: "to settle an agreement between two parties". To settle an agreement infers that there is a disagreement, or opposing desires or goals involved. Now bring this into the context of our heart where we have all experienced a disagreement between what God says, and the opposing desires of our flesh. He speaks to us about something and we don't want to do it, or we don't want to stop whatever it is we are doing. Father points out a path before us, but we hem and haw about how it doesn't fit into our own plans, schedule, or likes. Good seed, bad seed. Seed of the Spirit, seed of the flesh.

In the moment, self-will and compromise don't seem like such a big thing. After all, we are engulfed in a world that lives for self! It's not a hideous *beast* from which we, as *beauties*, recoil. Instead, we see its finer points and embrace it. We are attracted to it. We love it—fangs and all. But God calls His children to be holy as He is holy. Holy means "set apart"—set apart *for* God, set apart *from* our own self-centered ways. Set apart through love that doesn't compromise.

**Compromise is the cultivating of another seed in a garden intended for God's pleasure.** It engages with the corrupting current of fear, deception, and greed, empowered by a heart that listens to them. Jesus never compromised. Compromise is the antithesis of holiness because it seeks a mutual settlement between our holy spirit-man and the spirit of the world.

Paul addressed the Christians at Corinth (who were having all kinds of compromise-with-their-flesh issues) saying:

"Or what agreement has the temple of God with idols? For we are the temple of the living God; just as God said, 'I WILL DWELL IN THEM AND WALK AMONG THEM; AND I WILL BE THEIR GOD, AND THEY SHALL BE MY PEOPLE. Therefore, COME OUT FROM THEIR MIDST AND BE SEPARATE,' says the Lord. 'AND

DO NOT TOUCH WHAT IS UNCLEAN; And I will welcome you. And I will be a father to you, and you shall be sons and daughters to Me,' says the Lord Almighty" (2 Cor. 6:16-18).

Our heart is not only God's garden, but it is His temple, His dwelling place. An "idol" refers to anything we esteem more valuable than Him. "Idolatry" is the *act of our devotion* to it, contrary to what God is telling us. It sits in the place designed for devotion to God.

Jesus said, **"No man can serve two masters; for either he will hate the one, and love the other; or else he will be devoted to the one, and despise the other. You cannot serve God and wealth"**—Jesus (Matt. 6:24). We cannot serve God *and* our flesh, God *and* the spirit of the world, or God *and* greed. They are opposing natures.

Remember, any seeds—*inappropriate to our identity as Abba Father's sons and daughters*—that are *allowed* to grow in the ecosystem of our heart create what Scripture calls a *"neglected"* garden, a place that grows two different kinds of seed. A neglected garden is a *war zone* where every seed vies for existence, where two opposing dominions try to co-inhabit. It creates chaos in the soul!

The thorny vines of the spirit of the world, given permission by our flesh, have an agenda—the destructive agenda of their father, the liar and fear-monger.

*Worries* are lies because they do not reflect the power of God. They are loveless, peaceless, joyless thorns that press our mind with Godless thinking. **Wealth is deceptive** with the lie that pictures power and happiness as being rooted in possessions and positions, all the while subject to a world system not governed by divine wisdom, but markets that are swayed by speculations and greed. And *worldly pleasures* are also a lie—promising fulfillment if we satisfy some voice of lust; but in so doing, we find not a fulfillment of destiny, but bondage in a cage of thistles from which we long to escape.

The message of a lie promotes compromise, and thus bondage. And the spirit that nurtures the lie is fear.

## THE THORNY VINES OF FEAR

" . . . that through death He might render powerless him who had the power of death, that is, the devil, and might free those who through fear of death were subject to slavery all their lives" (Heb. 2:14b, 15).

Fear reigns where divine love is absent. It creates a perspective that the root of happiness is in the temporal, and that personal fulfillment comes through *self*-gratification—and that these can be taken at any moment, by any means. The definition of "fear" is: an *apprehension of impending danger accompanied with a desire to ward off the anticipated evil.* It brings *disorder* and *derangement.* Fear is the effect of guilt, and guilt denotes a debt incurred by an offense, crime, or violation of law (whether intentional or accidental), or a voluntary neglect of known duty. Guilt renders a person a debtor to the law, as it binds him to pay a penalty. Guilt therefore implies both criminality and liableness to punishment.

Fear isn't merely a feeling or mental state. It is a demonic spirit— an unseen but very real entity that preys on mankind to ensnare us. We see how this spirit preyed on Adam and Eve in the garden to engage deception and disobedience. And when Divine Love came looking for them, the fear now rooted in their heart could not reciprocate the fellowship of Divine Light. So they hid. And since that dreadful day, fear has become a "norm" for living in this world, a "norm" of darkness that we often don't recognize, but it's seen in our compromises.

The rich young ruler didn't recognize it either; what he did recognize was an anticipated evil at a loss of status and stash of goods should he follow Christ. Fear uses both real and perceived expectations to entrap us.

**"For it is He who delivers you from the snare of the trapper, and from the deadly pestilence"** (Ps. 91:3). The King James Version says *"noisome pestilence"*—noisome being "harmful to the senses," and in this case, the harm done to our spiritual senses, shutting us down from hearing God and perceiving Him. Spiritual senses that are shut down means a spiritual life shut down, thus impacting our fruitfulness as God's children. You get the picture.

### 1) Fear strangles our heart with cares

"Cares" are an anxiety (worry or stress) that is triggered by a sense of anticipated danger or lack. The problem here is that cares veil the eyes from seeing God with us, when God Himself says that **His eyes go to and fro throughout the whole earth to show Himself strong in behalf of those whose heart is completely His** (2 Chron. 16:9). Fear listens to the world's report instead of God's report. It strangles the seed of trust in God. The circumstance may be real, but there is a greater reality—God's ability *and* desire to care for you.

**"Cast all your cares on Him for He cares for you"** (1 Pet. 5:7).

He is Jehovah-jireh (God who provides) who promises to take care of all our needs as we seek His Kingdom first (Matt. 6:33). Jesus taught the people that just as the lilies of the field don't worry about their health, or the birds what they will eat, so God takes care of us, too. He cares for every detail of our life.

Paul told Timothy that no soldier entangles himself with the cares of this world so he can please the One who called him into service; our heart and mind cannot become intertwined with anxieties lest we be derailed from our heavenly service on earth. Remember, we ARE in a battle!

### 2) Fear strangles our heart with the deceitfulness of riches

This prickly touch infects the heart with internal disorder, eliciting a false arrangement of priorities to pursue wealth as the source of power, fulfillment, and perhaps even as a secret means of paying off the penalty of personal guilt. It blinds the eyes of justice with a bribe; turning law to lawlessness. It destroys individuals, families, corporations and nations with greed. It perverts governments with corruption, turning the heart as hard as the "precious metal" it seeks. It worships and trusts in the power of earthly gold, rather than the One who created it!

**"I pray that the eyes of your heart may be enlightened, so that you will know what is the hope of His calling, what are the *riches* of the glory of His inheritance in the saints,"** (Eph. 1:18 emphasis mine).

### 3) Fear strangles our heart with lust for pleasure

This fear chokes the heart with a sense of not being satisfied.

Its thorn pushes the heart to pursue inordinate pleasure and *uncontrolled gratification* through:

- Physical appetites of food and sex
- Intellectual appetites for entertainments and knowledge
- Emotional fulfillment in status and people's affirmation (or supression of needs by drugs or alcohol)
- Spiritual intimacy in Satanic worship and false gods

Lust indulges the affections outside the boundaries of how Father says we are to live. It replaces divine love with other loves . . . then guilt joins the crowd and deepens lust with shame. The book of Jude says that the increase of lust is a mark of the end-times.

King David who himself fell in adultery, came to understand that the deepest place of our heart can only be satisfied by God, and a full return to being in His image. When the heart feels satisfied, everything else falls into place. David said, **"I shall be satisfied when I awake in Your likeness"** (Ps. 17:15 NKJV).

God's Holy Word says:

"For where jealousy and selfish ambition exist, there is *disorder* and every evil thing. . . . As obedient children, do not be conformed to the former lusts which were yours in your ignorance . . . lusts that wage war against the soul. . . . Flee youthful lusts! . . . Pursue righteousness and do not let sin reign through obedience to your lusts. . . . Lay aside the old self that is corrupt through lusts . . . for we also once were foolish ourselves, disobedient, deceived, enslaved to various lusts and pleasures, spending our life in malice and envy,

hateful, hating one another. . . . But put on the Lord Jesus
Christ and make no provision for the flesh in regards to its
lusts. . . . Be filled with the Spirit! . . . The world is passing
away and its lusts, but the one who does the will of God lives
forever" (James 3:16; 1 Pet. 1:14; 1 Pet. 2:11; 2 Tim. 2:22; Eph.
4:22; Tit. 3:3; Rom. 13:14; Eph. 5:18; 1 John 2:17).

The Apostle Peter declared that if we have escaped the pollutions
of the world through the intimate knowledge of Christ and become
entangled again, our latter end will be worse than the former (2
Peter 2:20)! I don't know about you, but I never want to go back to
what I was in darkness.

Fear has many faces, but the bottom line is that fear is an absence
of love, an absence of the presence of God in our heart, our thoughts,
our focus. Paul wrote to Timothy saying, **"For God has not given us
a spirit of fear, but of power, and of love, and of a sound mind"** (2
Tim. 1:7). And John, after his revelation on the isle of Patmos wrote
to the Church: **"There is no fear in love; but perfect love casts out
fear, because fear involves punishment, and he who fears is not
perfected in love"** (1 John 4:18).

Do you feel entangled with worry, the deceit of riches, or worldly
pleasures?

**"It was for freedom that Christ set us free; therefore keep
standing firm and do not be subject again to a yoke of slavery"**
—Paul (Gal. 5:1).

## THE SEED, THE SNARES, AND THE SLOTHFUL
Weeds are not a one-time battle in our garden. They plague

our minds and thus our abilities, talents, and gifts, stopping fruitfulness that glorifies Father. While we can mark specific moments of inner-healing, needed breakthroughs, and wonderful deliverances in our life, weeds present a constant pervasive attack from the fallen world we live in coupled with a human nature attracted to its lure. Anyone who owns any plot of land knows the story: weed seeds come from all sides—currents of air carry them, birds drop them, animals track them, and they sneak in under fences through crawling root systems. They intrude and we must take action against their intrusion!

So how do we battle them? We disable compromise by *practicing* intimacy with God; we dispel fear by the *practice* of experiencing God's love; we discern lies by the *practice* of knowing truth—what truth sounds like, feels like, smells like, tastes like. Jesus overcame the devil's temptations in the wilderness with the intimate knowledge of His Father's words of truth. He met every challenge with "It is written. It is written. It is written."

**"You will know the truth and the truth will make you free."** —Jesus (John 8:32). Free from what? Free from the devil's snares and our flesh that agrees with him!

Ask anyone who has an addiction of any kind—how it started with desire but became their demise, a life ruining master, a cage from which they would give anything to be free. I know this from personal experience—gleefully picking up the first shiny link that soon became a heavy chain, not of adorning gold around my neck, but of iron around my feet and life—until God's love, truth, and power set me free.

Wise King Solomon understood the snares that people encounter. He knew how bad seed can strangle good seed. He was concerned for the garden of his own children's heart. He knew they would face many battles in life—wars of Satan against their destiny and fruitfulness as a righteous person and child of God. He wanted them to succeed. And so he wrote the book of Proverbs under the inspiration of the Holy Spirit—words of unprecedented wisdom.

**In it he wrote how the field of the slothful is a field of thorns and broken down hedges, where there is no understanding— and that it leads to poverty; that thorns and snares are in the way of the perverse, but the one who *keeps* his soul will be far from them"** (Prov. 24:30-31; 22:5).

These words weren't just for Solomon's sons, but for all people. God builds His house with wisdom, and wisdom's voice cries out to be heard! Are we listening? It calls to the simple to receive the Father's counsel in *all* things. It beckons us as Abba's children to seek understanding, *apply* truth, and listen to Father above the world's noisy enticements calling to our self-centeredness.

Here is truth: worldly weeds rob us of power, but God's wisdom gives us power to grow in who He created us to be. Wisdom trains us to be alert and diligent—not slothful, lazy, and apathetic— regarding thorns and snares, which Scripture says *bring a person to poverty.* Poverty is what the wicked look like, not the children of God. And I'm not talking about money. You can have this world's wealth and still be poor—lacking in the riches of Christ's love, peace, and joy.

This world's wealth is temporary. Jesus offered the rich young ruler a greater destiny, a greater wealth than what the world could offer him, but he couldn't see it. Jesus modeled for us that the greatest riches are the eternal ones (James 1:11).

Solomon also warned his sons specifically to *keep their soul* away from seductions—away from the lure of fornication and adultery. These destroy the soul with a destruction that ripples into the family, community, and nation. Without vigilance, the heart becomes like a harbor that ports every ship of disorder and evil (James 3:14-16). **But the heart was created to harbor one ship alone—the ship of God's presence and all the rich provision it provides.**

How would you describe your heart? Wealthy? Poor?

## HABITATION OF DRAGONS

 Now the prophet Isaiah described the place that is filled with thorns and thistles as a *"habitation of dragons"* (Isa. 34:13 KJV). That portrays it as being a *nesting ground for the demonic to live and lay their eggs.* Yikes!

I can certainly attest to that truth. When I was younger, my heart was an unkempt garden full of thorns, thistles . . . and dragons. And I was a Christian! I attended Bible School and went to church. Regularly. I was also addicted to tobacco, drank alcohol as oft and heavy as I could, smoked pot, and ran around with people who, like me, had no vision except for the pleasure of the moment. Talk about a mixed garden! And I was miserable. I'm thankful to the Heavenly Gardener who worked faithfully, unceasingly, in my heart to remove the imprisoning weeds and oust the dragons.

The spirit of the world has one goal regarding our heart: chain it with other loves and imprison the soul as a habitation of dragons so that the life of the spirit-man cannot flourish. Satan is at war over the harvest intended for your life and mine. He wants to make it what Proverbs calls a *"worthless"* garden—one that is fruitless ground. Thank God for the Father, Son, and Holy Spirit who work with us to make us *"blessed"*—a garden where His seed brings forth fruit in our life that glorifies Him.

## TAKING INVENTORY

The mind of the flesh swirls with worries, concerns of wealth, and pursuits of pleasures—**thoughts and imaginations that must be pulled down from their lofty controlling thrones!** Paul instructed the early church that it is *our* responsibility to take every thought captive and MAKE it OBEDIENT to Christ (2 Cor. 10:4-6). Yes, I said it, the "O" word—obedience. Our flesh hates obedience; it loves independence. But maturity in our life can only come through obedience to God, obedience that is empowered by the Holy Spirit. Paul said that the word of the Lord is sent to bring the nations (beginning with us) to the OBEDIENCE of faith (Rom. 16:26). Both true obedience and true faith spring from one root—divine love.

How will we one day rule the nations as God says we will, if we can't rule over our own flesh? How will we rule with the Heavenly Bridegroom if we are in love with another? With our own pursuits?

Worries, wealth, and worldliness can be comfortable. Double-mindedness can be comfortable, just ask the rich young ruler who, though momentarily sad, was more comfortable in choosing a life without Christ than a life without his wealth. And I bet he was still a religious man! Apathy toward God is comfortable for our flesh. Going with the flow of the world is comfortable. Even poverty and fear can be comfortable . . . too familiar to want change.

Compromise is comfortable because no one has to die, namely, our flesh. A neglected garden is comfortable because no one has to cultivate it, prune it, weed it, or develop it. No one has to take the time to bring it into the presence of God where the heart can be changed by His glory.

**"I have been crucified with Christ; and it is no longer I who live, but Christ lives in me; and the life which I now live in the flesh I live by faith in the Son of God, who loved me and gave Himself up for me"** (Gal. 2:20).

The bride in Song of Solomon said, **"Let my beloved come into his garden and eat his pleasant fruits"** (Song of Sol. 4:16). She wanted a garden that would satisfy *him,* not one where the harvest had failed.

Jesus *purposed* His life to be a beautiful garden for His Father's delight. He had a harvest that He wanted to see come to full fruition. He suffered in the flesh and died on a cross that we, too, might be clothed with that same purpose—no longer fearful and unbelieving, or living for our own lusts, but for the will of the Father.

*He wore a crown of thorns that we might wear the victor's crown.*

What are the cares, concerns for wealth, or worldly pleasures that are strangling spiritual maturity in your life? Pulling you away from intimacy with Christ and faith in God? Be honest.

True success can only happen when you are honest with God, and yourself, about the condition of your heart. What fear is secretly ensnaring you? Pray and ask the Holy Spirit to show you those areas and what you should do. Make a list of each and also what He says to do. (1 John 1:7-9)

**Worries tell me:**_____

**Wealth tells me:** _____

**Worldly pleasures say:** _____

**God calls me to:** _____

*Father, forgive me for where I have worried and not trusted You, where I have sought money more than seeking You, and where I have spent my time more on pleasures than laboring with You for Your harvest in the earth, as a true son or daughter. I now join with You in removing the unrighteous seeds rooted in my affections, will, and emotions. I want every thorn, thistle, and dragon removed from my heart. Make my heart pure—every thought, action, and motive. Search my heart and remove every wicked way in me, every area of compromise. You are worthy of the fruit that You desire from my life. I love you Father, in Jesus name. Amen.*

# 7

## THE FRUITFUL LIFE: HEARING GOD

*"And those are the ones on whom seed was sown on the good soil; and they hear the word and accept it and bear fruit, thirty, sixty, and a hundredfold."*
*—Jesus (Mark 4:20)*

Okay, we've looked at things that Jesus said will stop a seed's destiny. In the next few chapters, we are going to look at three *specific* elements that the most successful Man says will nurture God's seed in you to full harvest. Every living thing requires certain elements for life and growth. Cultivating a seed from planting to harvest takes time and intentional actions.

According to Jesus, bringing God's word and purpose in our life to fruitfulness requires this condition of the heart:

1. **It hears God's words**
2. **It accepts (holds on to) what God says**
3. **It bears fruit with perseverance**

These three conditions empower and mature the valuable seed of who you are as a child of God—spiritually, naturally, and in every way.

In this chapter, we are going to look at the first condition for a fruitful life: hearing God.

But first, a story.

## THE FAITH TRAVELER

Young Abram moved briskly through the market square, in a hurry to gather last minute preparations for their journey. It was a sultry day. Walking through the market square, nearing the Temple of Nanna, he stopped in front of the idol maker's shop. A cool breeze from nowhere rushed past him.

"I am not known by a form," whispered a Voice.

"I know. Oh, how I know." He muttered under his breath.

At his father's request, Abram entered the old establishment to buy a small carving of Nanna, Ur's celebrated diety. Abram's father, Terah, wanted to make sure their upcoming move was safe. The statue of Nanna, the moon god, would watch over them—as well as the Creator God (Elohim), of course—as they travelled to Canaan. Abram cringed as he picked up the idol. Hmm, eyes that don't see. Ears that don't hear. How great father Shem (who had come through the famous flood so long ago) would despise such an action. Abram came from a family line that had taught each generation of a faith in the one Creator God—and no other. But Terah's heart was not so devoted to One. He was, how do you say, "open minded" to the practices of the society in which they lived.

Abram thought about Eber, too (Shem's son), whose devotion to Elohim as the only true God, won him notoriety as one who refused to help build Nimrod's tower to heaven at Babel a few years after

114

the great flood. Abram had a heritage from strong men of faith, descendents of Noah who himself stood alone as a preacher of righteousness before the historical deluge—the judgment waters that nearly destroyed all life on earth.

But Terah was different than his forefathers. Perhaps influenced by the culture of Ur, he had no affinity regarding Elohim, but sought the favor of all acknowledged deities. He believed that all roads lead to heaven.

Plans of moving to Canaan had been in the making for a long time. After the great father Noah and his sons had left Mt. Ararat when the flood waters dried up, Shem made his way to the plain of Shinar. There he remained, but his heart envisioned another place—a place that God revealed to Him. It was this particular land for which Shem named his son, Eber, meaning: *"the region beyond."* Eber's name spoke of the region *beyond the Euphrates,* south and westward. Shem's naming of Eber was a prophetic declaration of the purposes of God for his legacy and lineage. It was, however, also the place where Canaan (Shem's nephew who had been cursed by father Noah) had, by now inhabited and settled.

Seven generations had now passed with the family still in Shinar. But now, Terah felt the stirrings of the prophetic word within him. It was time. He would pick up his family and begin the aged quest—his heart awakened, perhaps, by the tragic and untimely death of his youngest son, Haran.

Abram returned with his undesirable purchase as the family finished loading up their goods. At last they set out on the long journey, following the flood plain that lay beside the River Euphrates.

They travelled until they came to the border city of Haran. Like Ur, Haran was an advanced cultural city of its day, as well as a worship center of pagan gods. Whether a fear of danger in travelling the unfamiliar *region beyond*, or the lifestyle that Haran's culture could provide, or perhaps that the city's name itself reminded him of his dead son, Terah stopped and went no further. There he remained with his family until the day of his death.

Perhaps it wasn't such a coincidence that Terah's very name meant: *delay*. The seed of destiny was in him, but the love of other gods made him drag his feet in following Elohim. He never made it to Canaan, nor saw a divine destiny in the promised land.

At Terah's death, the seventy year old Abram was now head of the family clan. Taking a walk in the nearby hills, he paused, looking southward. The moon was bright. The sky lit with brilliant stars—numerous as the sands by the sea.

A familiar Voice spoke.

"Abram, I want you to leave this place, and go to a land that I will show you. I will make of you a great nation—I will bless you and make your name great, and you will be a blessing. I will bless those that bless you and curse those who curse you. In you all the families of the earth will be blessed."

The delay was over. It was time to move forward—to cultivate the seed of destiny. Abram's spirit flooded with new vision—visions of a city, unlike Ur and Haran with all their worldly splendor, but one whose builder and maker was God, the God who speaks with men. The God who sees. The God who hears prayer. Elohim was calling him into a purpose and blessing that involved the whole earth.

Abram was the *eighth* generation from Eber and the tenth from Noah—a perfect time for the ending of an old era, and the beginning of a new one. It was time for the seed of destiny in a family line to be planted in the place of God's choosing, in soil that would one day bring forth a Seed for a *world* harvest. And who was chosen to engage the small beginning of this infinite purpose? The one whose faith would make him known throughout history as the *"friend of God"*.

Abram left Haran, taking Sarai and his nephew, Lot, and entered the region beyond—Canaan. Pitching his tent as he moved, he journeyed all the rest of his days, following God from place to place, until by the end of his life he had walked all the land that God had showed him. The stories of his walk with God are written and still being rehearsed throughout the world. His trust and love for Elohim has given him the title as *"the father of all those who believe."* So great was his relationship with God that even his name was changed to Abraham: Abram + **Ha**shem (God). Sarai's name, too, was changed to Sarah: Sarai + **Ha**shem.

Abraham became the father of a living faith that bears fruit through intimate devotion to the "speaking God"—to the Holy Father who calls His sons and daughters into a destiny by which the whole earth is blessed.

Abraham listened to God, accepted what He said, and carried it in his heart and choices until that word came to full fruition in his life. Was he a perfect man? No. But he never stopped listening to God and putting action to his faith.

## HEAVEN'S SECRET: GOOD SOIL LISTENS TO GOD

We know that we are hearing God by our movement in response to what He says to us. Hearing is defined as the ability to receive and process communication, and then reciprocate a response. Communication requires knowing the same language in some form or another. Otherwise, there is no exchange of information. **As God's child, if all we hear and experience is the voice of an earthly realm, then all we know is what a fallen earth tells us.** God greatly desires that we hear and understand His communication with us.

Terah felt a desire to move to Canaan. He began to move in response to what, I believe, was a generational call of God coming down the family line regarding a promised land. There is a lot of talk about generational curses, but there needs to be more understanding of generational blessings! The word of God's purpose moved within Terah, but his love for other gods plugged his ear so that he didn't understand the divine call on his lineage, and thus, it never grew to fruition in his life. But Abraham's heart toward God was fertile soil, good soil that received the call with clarity.

Terah didn't discern the deception of the spirit of this world—a spirit that lures the heart with intentions to kill the maturing of divine purpose in a person's life. He didn't discern how it works to abort our destiny by our own choices, replacing our God-given identity with a corrupt one, and cloaking our potential with a veil of ignorance.

We have an adversary who works diligently, constantly, angrily to keep us from hearing God and moving with His voice. He is afraid that we might understand the value of who we are in Christ's image. He trembles lest we take our rightful authority that was won back for us at the cross. God's voice reveals to us His heart and kind intentions toward us. And just like we know people by their words, God's words helps us to know Him, as He really is—not what the devil (who hurls accusations and judgments) says of Him. And in knowing God, we know who we are too.

We don't *typically* hear God with our natural ears, but with our *spiritual* ears. *Spiritual ears* refer to the ability of our spirit-man to connect with the voice of God. Even when we hear His voice through others' words, we are not merely hearing with our natural ears, but with our spiritual ears that are picking up the *sound* of His voice. **Ears are the channel by which we receive faith.** And just as Jesus experienced in life on earth, the Holy Spirit is our Helper and Teacher who aids us in hearing God, and knowing His language. God's voice conveys His heart and purpose for our life, family, and work.

Children—young lives full of latent potential—need teachers. Our Divine Teacher (the *Helper* from the Father) is also called the *Spirit of the Son*, because He imparts to us the things of the Son. He trains you and me to grasp what true sonship is, what it looks like, and how it is lived out in power!

Our ability to hear is developed through intimate relationship with the Holy Spirit. He teaches us to recognize the sound of God's voice. Remember when you first heard the gospel and your heart was moved to action? That was the Holy Spirit causing you to hear truth and respond to it! Then you got hungry to know that Voice more and so you started reading the Bible.

God's written Word is the foundation for *everything* else we hear

119

from God. As we meditate in the **Holy Scriptures**, the Heavenly Mentor *breathes* on them to reveal the mind of God in them to the mind of our spirit-man. It's like He causes the words to jump off that page and right into our heart!

Hebrews 4:12 describes God's voice contained in His Word as being **living and active, sharper than a two-edged sword to pierce between spirit and soul, able to judge the thoughts and intents of the heart.** His truth is a divine energy for growth, a weapon of war for the battle of the heart, and a righteous judge of our thought life. God's living words refresh our spirit, renew our mind, and restore our soul.

## THE ART OF LISTENING

In Hebrews 3, the Divine Teacher addresses our nature as children who are too often preoccupied, distracted, and not listening. He says, **"... Today, if you hear His voice, do not harden your hearts ..."** (Heb. 3:7-8a NIV). There are three parts to what the Holy Spirit just said here about listening to God (and in specific reference to Jesus, who the world rejects):

1. **Today**—not tomorrow, next week, next year, when you feel like it, when it's convenient....you know the excuses

2. **If you hear *His voice***—hearing is a capacity; listening is a choice

3. **Do not harden your heart**—don't make it difficult for His word to take root—a hard heart means one that is stubborn, unwilling, independent

The Teacher says that hearing is: a *"now"* thing, a choice to listen, and a choice of *how* we respond to what God says. Important note: *"now"* prepares us for tomorrow. Choosing to listen means practicing a healthy relationship with God, and having a tender heart that acts on what He says.

What has God spoken to you? Have you been acting on the revelation given you? What is Jesus saying to you now, today? Are you listening? And if you are, how are you responding?

**We listen in different ways:**

1.  Active listening—I'm all ears! Yes, Sir!
2.  Passive listening—Oh, I'm sorry, I forgot what you said, I'll get to it . . . soon.
3.  Selective listening—Uh-huh. Mm-hmm. You said what?
4.  Not listening—Lalalalalalala.

Which one of these is most prevalent in your relationship with the Father, Son, and Holy Spirit? Be honest. Remember, we are children on a journey learning to hear better, listen better, and respond better. Children are basically self-centered and have to learn to listen closely and respond rightly. **Listening and responding appropriately** to parents, and to God, is an act of love.

The word *Hear (Grk. Akouo)* means: to perceive sound sensation, to *listen* (as to a teacher) for the purpose of learning and understanding, considering what is said, and perceiving the *sense* of what is said. The **antonym** of hearing is: to be dull, deaf.

Job 34:3 says, **"For the ear tests words as the palate tastes food."** The hearing that God speaks of isn't merely the capacity to perceive sound vibrations, but is the ability to taste words, discern their savor with understanding to either assimilate its content for nourishment and enjoyment, or spit it out if it's bad. Testing words is important because you can't believe everything you hear! We live in a world of words and messages. What messages are we swallowing that need to be spit out? What words are we leaving on the plate that need to be eaten?

God further defines hearing as listening with understanding and **action.** To not do what you hear is to not have heard at all . . . to not have listened.

**"Then He said to me, 'Son of man, eat what you find; eat this scroll, and go, speak to the house of Israel'"** (Ezek. 3:1).

What has God said to you, and what action did He want you to take?

Let's look at how God's Word links the ear and the heart together.

## THE EAR—BRAIN—HEART CONNECTION

Anatomically speaking, while the ear is the faculty that receives

sound vibration, it is actually the brain that processes and interprets sound waves as words and their meaning. **We hear sound with the ear and understand it with the brain.** It's one thing to hear a sound, it's another to understand it. You can talk to me all day long in a language I don't know and all I hear is blah, blah, blah. It will make no sense to me. The brain has to be trained to discern and interpret what the ear perceives. Just think about how much time a baby spends just listening and learning to understand the voice of its parents—the whole first year of its life!

**How much time do we spend with our Heavenly Father listening to Him, learning to know His voice, and understand His words?**

Now, go a step further in this process and we come to the **mind** (Grk. *Nous*)—the part within us that processes the sense of what the brain has interpreted. The mind is the seat of **reflective consciousness,** comprising the faculties of perception, understanding, feeling, judging and determining.

The mind refers to a *particular mode of thinking*. As born-again believers, we have three distinct minds that Holy Scripture talks about:

- The *natural mind*—what we just described as the reflective consciousness and its faculties, natural thought processes, impressions, emotions, and memories that carry patterns of belief systems and response systems.
- The *carnal mind*—the mind of the flesh and its self-centered passions.
- The *spiritual mind*—the conscious realm of our spirit man that receives the thoughts and impressions of the Holy Spirit.

There is one other mind, too: the *mind of the heart.* Medical science has discovered a heart-brain connection. They have found that the heart itself actually has a "brain"—a mind. God knew this way before modern science. Really. Proverbs 23:7 says that **as**

**a man thinks in his heart, so is he.** Once again we see King Solomon teaching his son about the heart, this time about its thinking processes.

Which "mind" is our heart thinking with? The natural one? Carnal one? Or spiritual one that we received at our new birth in Christ? We hear with our ears, interpret with our brain and think, not just with our mind, but with our heart. The mind and heart work together.

The *natural mind* interprets the every day occurrences of life through our *natural* senses, experiences, and acquired knowledge. It also interprets and processes life (people, circumstances, desires) through the appetites of our flesh, strongholds, biases, and environmental influences (influences that may be at enmity with God). Paul said that to the natural mind, the things of God are *foolishness*—it cannot comprehend them. That is why we are not to rely on our own natural understanding, but to be *acquainted* with God and He will teach us His perspective—a framework of truth and understanding that goes beyond what the natural mind knows or comprehends.

It is important to understand these different minds within us. Look at this: if we hear the voice of God with our spirit man, yet *process* it with the **natural mind,** His words may not make it to the planting field of the heart. Why? Because the natural mind doesn't understand it. Doesn't get it. It rejects the Word of God. It twists the Word of God. It denies the Word of God. It doesn't consider it. It hears God's voice as mere natural thunder rather than a divine message. It hears: blah, blah, blah.

If we process God's word with the *carnal mind,* it is sure to not get planted, because this mode of thinking is completely focused on self. *What will I get from this?* The truth is, every word we hear from God, or any other source, should be processed with the *mind of Christ,* that is, *the mind of the Spirit.* The mind of the Spirit has the only framework and perspective that is *fully* truth. That's why the demonic realm tries to keep us in the cycle of natural and carnal thinking. It gives them the opportunity to snatch, scorch, or strangle the divine seed from becoming fruitful in us.

Here's an example: after many years of being in church leadership, the pastor came to me one day and said he felt that the Lord wanted me to go on a sabbatical. I was taken aback as I had just recently heard the Lord speak something to me quite the opposite, a word that He confirmed to me. My natural mind struggled as I did not understand the situation, at all. And my carnal mind was just plain angry! I didn't want to go on a sabbatical. I loved church work and ministry. I loved being involved.

I went to bed that night upset. But while I slept (when I finally settled down enough to sleep), the Lord spoke to me in a dream. I heard Him say, "El-Roi." I woke up, and getting up quietly so as not to wake my husband, I went upstairs to pray. I felt to read the story of Hagar in the Old Testament—and there it was, the name El-Roi: the God who sees me. I read the passage and understood what He was saying. He saw my situation, but also wanted me to go back and submit to what the pastor had said on the matter of sabbatical. So I did.

I could have stayed angry, gotten bitter, or even left the church (responding by my natural or carnal mind). But I heard what God said and I moved on His words, and not on what my mind and emotions felt. And while the sabbatical seemed endless (three years), God did so much work in my heart and life during that time. Most importantly, I came to understand the divine value of rest. And when that season was over, God moved me into a new time where the prior word He had given me came into place.

Our Heavenly Gardener knows what He is doing, but only the mind of the Spirit understands that and is able to engage with God for His purposes. The natural and carnal mind only see circumstances, and perceive only how self is impacted.

And here's the great news! **We *have* the mind of Christ!** It just needs to be used. As Abba Father's children, we have spiritual receptors to see, hear, touch, taste, discern and experience God *and* His world through the mind of the Spirit. The joy is in learning to listen and discern His words, learning the impressions of the Holy Spirit (that we receive through our spiritual senses)—letting the thought processes that are fitting and harmonious with Father's nature form us, shape our mindsets, and redefine our mode of thinking. The Holy Spirit "re-wires" our mode of thinking so that we understand by the Spirit, rather than by the soul.

In A. B. Simpson's book, *Walking in the Spirit* (Holy Spirit Christian Classics), he writes:

> *"'What man knoweth the things of a man, save the spirit of man which is in him? Even so the things of God knoweth no man, but the Spirit of God' (1 Cor. 2:11). You might sit down and talk to your little dog about the latest book, and explain to him in the clearest manner its wonderful teachings, and he would not understand a*

*word; not from any defect in the truth, but because he had not the mind of a man to understand the things of a man; and so you might sit down and talk to the natural intellect about spiritual truth, even the brightest human intellect, and it would not comprehend it because it belonged to a higher sphere.*

*The only way by which the dog could understand you would be for you to impart to him a human mind, and the only way that man can understand the things of God is for God to impart to him the divine mind."*

## LISTENING WITH THE MIND OF CHRIST

The mind of Christ thinks like the Father and the Spirit—not in religious prose, but in holy and divine truth. It is an **anointed** (Grk: *Christos*) mind. **Anointed means: smeared with oil.** In Psalm 23, David said that the Lord *anointed* his head with oil when he was going through a really difficult time—it was a protective balm against the thoughts the enemy brings. Shepherds smear oil on sheep's heads to keep flies (representing demonic activity) from laying their eggs in the sheep's brain and driving them crazy. Literally.

Have you ever felt like your mind was driving you crazy? Mm-hmm, me too. Those are called dark thoughts: unrest, confusion, worry, rage. And they always revolve around one specific thing . . . me. **But the anointed mind—Christ's mind—brings peace and a sound mind—one that is not troubled or shaken, because it's thought patterns are *fixed* on God, seeing Him and His ability** (2 Thess. 2:2; 1 Pet. 1:13; Isa. 26:3).

The Anointed One (Jesus) is called the Prince of Peace. His mind is undisturbed. It has "light-filled thoughts" not dark thoughts. No vain imaginations, fantasies, rejection issues, false judgments, accusations, offenses, or intimidations. His mind isn't all wrapped up in Himself, or what someone said or did to Him. He isn't distracted by unhealthy emotions; nor is His mind laden with shame or condemnation. He is at peace, perfect peace.

It is said that peace is the "potting soil" for the revelation of God because God's voice is best heard when we are at peace, no matter what is going on around us.

The anointed mind of Christ is also one of **power**. David declared that the Lord *empowered* him, anointing him with fresh oil (Ps. 92:10). Oil is a form of energy supply—power! Thoughts that are anointed and full of light are thoughts with power, thoughts such as, **"I can do all things through Him who strengthens me"** (Phil. 4:13). The anointing of the Holy Spirit empowers *how* we think, which enables us to more effectively minister to others by His mind, rather than reacting by our flesh. **Darkness likes to attach itself to how we think.**

Oil is also a **healing** energy. An anointed mind is a healed mind—healed from past wounds and unhealthy emotional responses. Healing is important to the success of our destiny. There are many anointed ministries in the Body of Christ who help bring such healing by the Spirit and godly counsel. Get help if you need it. It will help get you free from the internal places of the soul where you are being held captive or unfruitful.

So we see that the mind of the Spirit empowers us to hear clearly, think like Father, and respond accordingly. This is essential for us as Abba's children who are children of Light. *How we hear and think is how we will respond to God, circumstances, and to one another, and even how we respond to ourselves.*

Here are some other descriptions of the mind of Christ:

1. **It thinks with love**—"This is the covenant that I will make with them . . . I will put My laws on their heart and on their mind I will write them" (Heb. 10:16). The sum of God's laws is the fulfillment of love (1 Tim. 1:5).

2. **It thinks with humility**—"Let this mind be in you which was in Christ Jesus . . . who humbled himself to death, even the death of the cross" (Phil. 2:5-8).

3. **It thinks with passion for God and His Kingdom**—not settings its affections on things of the earth (Col. 3:2).

4. **It thinks on good things**—it *practices* thinking on what is true honorable, right, pure, lovely, of good report, excellent and praise worthy (Phil. 4:8).

A *restful spirit* is also the evidence of the mind of Christ. Paul said that on his journey with God, he had learned to be content in all things (Phil. 4:11). Rest is part of divine fruitfulness. Disturbed emotions can hinder our hearing and cause internal chaos, but the thoughts of the Spirit are restful ones needed in uneasy times.

I hope you are getting this. How we think directly corresponds with how we hear, how we listen, how we respond. The mind of Christ listens to the Father and the Comforter. His mind in us processes life with thinking that is congruent with the nature of God (His love, goodness, etc). This empowers our thoughts to convey the *emotions* of God's presence—joy! The mind of Christ thinks outside the box of the earthly realm—beyond the organic, beyond natural resources. It sees God's ability greater than our own inability. It looks to God for supernatural wisdom for natural problems. It sees God as the source of provision. It thinks life not death!

David said, **"Your word I have hidden in my heart so that I might not sin against You"** [meaning: won't err from You—Ps. 119:11 NKJV]. God's words were important to David. He lived the same life realities that we all experience, understanding that if something isn't important to us, our mind dismisses it. But if we consider it valuable, we'll think about it. And the more we think about it, the more *place* it holds in our mind and heart. Doing so, it then becomes the reality by which we live.

What we hear become thoughts, ideas, imaginations, intentions . . . and these shape our life. That's why we are told to grab those swirling vain thoughts that are contrary to God's thoughts and bring them to the obedience of the Son. Personally, this has been a learning process of the Holy Spirit with me for many years—recognizing dark thoughts, no matter what shade of gray, breaking agreement with it, and bringing my thoughts to obey the light of truth.

Listening and thinking God's way of thinking builds a life that loves Him with all the heart, soul, mind, and strength.

So here it is. We aren't born in God with spiritual ears that can't hear Him. We just have to get rid of the distractions, learn to listen, learn God's language, and learn with the mind of Christ.

Good thing we have a Teacher!

## VOICE RECOGNITION AND MOVEMENT

Earlier we defined the opposite of the hearing ear as one that is "dull". In Scripture, dullness is not an inability to hear, but one of capacity that's not being used. We were born of God to function with an unction, not dysfunction with no unction!

A *dull* (or deaf) ear is one that is insensitive in its perception of sound—it doesn't respond. Throughout the Old Testament, God continually corrected His children (Israel) for not being sensitive to His voice—they didn't take action on the revelation He gave them. **Doing what God says is His definition of hearing.**

Now look here. Jesus said, **"My sheep hear My voice, and I know them, and they follow Me"** (John 10:27). They hear and take action! You were born of God with NO dysfunction. Did you hear that? So many Christians say, "I can't hear God." Did you hear Him pull your heart string to come to Christ in the first place? Then you CAN hear God. It's just a matter of learning to recognize His voice.

God speaks to us in many different ways. We may hear Him as a still small voice inside, an impression, a sense of knowing something, a picture we see and feel impressed with, a dream, a song that begins to resonate in our spirit, an idea, an unusual event or coincidence, an unexpected but timely encounter with someone who encourages us, a vision, a simple "awareness" of something, or Scriptures that the Holy Spirit "highlights" to our understanding. Even the very hunger that we have for God is His speaking, drawing us. And these are just a few ways we hear Him!

How do we know it's HIS voice? The more we practice voice recognition, the better we get at it. Look, if a modern man-made machine can do "voice recognition," how much more a living spiritual child with a speaking Divine Parent? And the more we practice moving on what we hear, the better our hearing is developed. And not just hearing and responding, but hearing correctly. The other day, I received a text message from a friend using her "voice recognition" application on her phone. What she said was, "I'm definitely going in a different direction." What her phone "heard" and sent me was "I'm deathly going in a different direction." I thought, *huh?* It is one thing to hear, and another to hear correctly! As we listen to the Holy Spirit, He will lead us into all truth.

When Jesus was on earth, He **practiced** listening to God and taking action (obedience) to the Spirit's leading. **He became an expert at discerning and moving on what He heard from God.** Some of the places where the Holy Spirit led Jesus included: spending time in intimate fellowship with Father, ministering to people, discipling those around Him, and just hanging out with others for relationship building, you know, dinner parties. The Holy Spirit also led Jesus to the desert to be tested of the devil, to the cross to be crucified, raised Him up from the grave, and then took Him to be seated with the Father. Sounds like an awesome journey to me! (Except the part about the devil or anything painful).

We can become skilled in hearing God, too, because we have spiritual ears just like Jesus had when He walked this earth. Yes, we do.

Our learning experience as Abba's children is a learning journey of listening and taking action. It's a new way of life for us, because our old way of living was accustomed to not hearing, and not responding. But hearing and moving with God makes the seed inside us resonate with energy, because it's living and active! It makes our spirit, as well as our gifts and talents, to come alive! Alive with dominion power and authority.

And by the way, Jesus told me one time that He LOVES dominion—the dominion of light, love, kindness, gentleness, faith, peace, joy, and self-control. Yep, that's what He said. He loves His Father's Kingdom on earth as it is in heaven.

So, having ears, we may be hearing but just not recognizing God's voice. OR . . . we may be hearing and *choosing* not to respond, for whatever reason. What do you mean? Many religious organizations (denominations) do not believe that God speaks today . . . or heals, or does miracles. Now, if I think He isn't speaking, I won't learn to listen. Instead, I will disregard whatever I am hearing from Him. My hearing will go undeveloped.

Other people believe God does speak, but only know His written Word *(logos)*; they haven't learned His spoken *(rhema)* voice. But in Matthew 4:4, Jesus says that people are to live on every *word* that proceeds from God's mouth; the "word" here is *"rhema"*. (Note: God's *rhema* will NEVER contradict His *logos*, and in fact, we hear His rhema through His logos.)

## THE DILEMMA OF DULL EARS

If we don't act on what we hear, we open ourselves to the spiritual disease of **dullness**. The prophet Isaiah describes the dull ear in God's children as being created by a *calloused heart full of* *fat.* Fat is a build-up of *stored oils*—an unhealthy excess due to too much consumption and not enough oil burning action. Did you hear that? Not enough *oil burning action* going on! This means not using the anointing that God has given to us. Taking it in, but not giving it out. This makes our hearing dull.

1 John 2:27 says that you have been given an anointing that remains in you—a well that you can always draw from. It's an anointing of the Spirit that *teaches you* as you go about your day, how to live in power, love, and wholeness. And not just that, but an anointing of the Spirit that wants to *flow out* through you to those around you as power to heal, encourage, cast out demons, raise the dead, give hope to the hopeless, and set oppressed souls free.

In the Old Testament, God's people had the signs and miracles of God, supernatural provision and visitation, continual God

 encounters, angelic ministry and divine counsel. **Their revelation of God was rich, but their faith output (action) was not consistent to their intake.** This made them dull in their life with God. If we could see our spirit man, what picture would we see? Is our new heart beating strong with the heartbeat of God's love and passions inside us? Are we hearing His thoughts clearly? Thinking with His mind? Are we using what He has given us? Is our output matching our intake?

People, cultures, and nations are waiting for the release of the anointing of the Lord in your life. Let it flow! Unstop the well! Pour out that Kingdom anointing over every area of personal need and

out to others. Don't let it be stagnant. Recognize it. Use it. Don't let it become like wax in the ears because of non-use.

**We need to deeply appreciate, and highly value, what God has given us through the Son by the Spirit.** Not using what God gives us creates a dysfunction in our hearing and life. James 1:22 says, **"But prove yourselves doers of the word, and not merely hearers who** *delude [deceive]* **themselves"** (emphasis and clarification mine from the Greek). That deception is what makes us forget how our new life in Christ began in the first place—at the cross, buried with Christ, and raised in new life by a divine act that we ourselves could never perform on our own. Our new life and identity in Christ is a precious gift from God, both as a blessing to us and others.

What has God said to you recently? Take Note! For when you receive one word from God and give it active empowered intention, it accelerates your ability to hear more.

Jesus wasn't giving us an impossible commission when He said to **"Heal the sick, cleanse the lepers, raise the dead, cast out devils: freely have you received, freely give"** (Matt. 10:8). Neither was He jesting when He declared, **"These signs will accompany those who have believed: in My name they will cast out demons, they will speak with new tongues; they will pick up serpents, and if they drink any deadly poison, it will not hurt them; they will lay hands on the sick, and they will recover"** (Matt. 16:17-18).

## WHAT HAS OUR EAR'S ATTENTION?

Sounds. We tune them in and tune them out. We live in a world that is a cacophony of noise, chatter, words, thoughts, and

135

perceptions that feed the mind and implore its considerations. Each of these herald some message—whether of love and hope, courage and strength, or another, such as jealousy, greed, rejection, or shame. Messages are seeds that seek a place to grow. That's why we must guard our heart with *all diligence*.

While these may or may not *vie* for our attention, one sound that makes our heart leap is the sound of someone we love. Whatever you love, you will give your greatest attention. The greatest careers are built on things to which people passionately give their talent and attention. Relationships are strongest when the heart and ear is engaged. Not listening to God and moving with Him isn't always so much a faith problem, as perhaps a love problem.

**"Have faith in God. . . . Faith that works by love"** (Mark 11:22; Gal. 5:6).

God has elevated love as the most important commandment for life: **"You shall love the Lord your God with all your heart, and with all your soul, and with all your mind"**—Jesus (Matt. 22:37). Love is the most important factor for hearing God: it turns the ear, engages the mind, and fills the heart. It is a relentless force, adamant in its desire. It counts the cost and sells all for the sake of the one it loves—like Jesus did for us . . . like we are to do for Him.

Everything about our relationship with God is experienced through a covenant of LOVE: a love bond between children and their Abba Father, between a bride and Bridegroom, between friends. Each of these is a type of relationship built through *intimate communication*. We long to hear Him because we love Him, because He loves us. We want to know what He is saying, what He is doing, what His heart desires. We want to know His counsel. It's important to us. He's important to us.

In my youth, I struggled in hearing God. I knew He loved me and I wanted to know Him. But the world had my attention. I had so many voices clamoring for my engagement: pain, rebellion, anger, fear, self-pity, self-will. You name it, I heard it. I didn't know how to love God in a way that stands up to the other voices and says, "I love just One! And I'm listening to Him!" My desires were for a lot of things, ungodly things, and they were distracting me, directing me in every way except toward God. I processed a lot of things with my carnal mind. Life was all about me. The seed of God within me was there but not growing, because I was too busy watering the messages from the spirit of the world, the wounds of my soul, and my fleshly desires . . . but I could hear its living voice crying for the Light.

## DESIRE *TURNS* OUR FACE TOWARD THE SPEAKER

We know by experience that when our heart *desires* relationship, then our head turns and our ear *wants* to listen. We desire to hear. A lover whispers in our ear, we listen. A friend shares their dream with us, we listen. A beloved parent advises us, we turn our face toward them so that our ear can hear their sound.

**"My son, if you receive my words . . . turning your ear to wisdom and applying your heart to understanding . . . then you will understand the fear of the Lord and find the knowledge of God"** (Prov. 2:1-5 NIV).

Now look at the opposite scenario. We quarrel with a loved one; they make us mad, we storm out of the room, or stay in the room but refuse to communicate. We don't want to hear their words. Or how about when we feel betrayed by a friend; we don't want to hear their dreams anymore, we want their apology. Or how about the ears that are covered by the hands of a self-willed child who is saying through this action, I'm not listening! These are what a face turned away from the speaker looks like.

**"Thus the Lord used to speak to Moses, face to face, just as a man speaks to his friend"** (Exod. 33:11).

*Desire* is the spark that turns the face toward the speaker—a desire to hear lest we miss what the loved one is saying, what the friend is sharing, what needed information might be revealed, or some wisdom that may change the course of our life. A spouse who cares about their marriage, cares to listen. A friend who cares about their friend, cares to listen. A student who cares about being educated listens because they desire to excel.

Not listening may not necessarily be the manifestation of a *lack* of desire (disinterest), it may be the result of distraction, busyness, or maybe some inner disturbance. These are things that need to be dealt with if we are to grow and succeed on our course of being fruitful.

Some of the ways that we turn our face toward God include: prayer, meditating on His Word, and fellowship with believers. Some of the ways that we turn our face away from God are: neglecting intimacy with Him in prayer and the Word, and isolating ourselves from Christian fellowship with brothers and sisters.

Is your face turned toward God? Or away from Him?

We opened this chapter with the story of a man who was distracted by the voices of a pagan culture, and perhaps even the grief over his son's death. But Abraham heard God, listened to Him and acted on what Elohim revealed to him. Eternity was in his heart. He had a destiny to walk in, and an identity with God to live out. He gave his heart to be rich soil in which the purposes of God could come to full fruition. And from his engagement with the voice of God came that which blessed the whole earth—Jesus Christ who was of the lineage of Abraham.

As we learn to give *our* heart as rich soil to the seed of God's voice—learning to recognize, listen, and move on what He says—who knows what blessing will come through our fruitfulness to enrich another. No matter if it seems to be just fruit for a few, in Jesus' hands a few is multiplied to feed thousands.

Be careful how you hear. Don't let a single divine thought escape your attention. No matter how ordinary or unassuming the whisper of that still small voice may seem, it carries a living destiny within it.

## LAB CLASS: HEARING GOD

Put it into practice. Pay attention. Take God's voice seriously. Take time to listen. What does Jesus tell you? How is the Holy Spirit leading you? What is Father saying? Make a list. Write it down. Use this lab class as a guide.

**What God is saying:** _____

**How I'm responding:** _____

**What I'm doing with it:** _____

Remember, as the brain empowers the body through electrical flow, the mind of Christ empowers the seed of identity. His thoughts fill you with the energy of Holy Spirit thinking. Here are some ways to practice getting out of your mind and into His, in order to help develop the holy seed within you.

- Break agreement with passivity—command it to get off your life. God is speaking to you and the seed of identity in you is HUNGRY for His voice. Feel the hunger. Get out of bed, out of your comfort zone, and go feed your spirit-man.

- Open the love letter He wrote for you (the Holy Bible). Read it! Meditate on it. Renew your mind with it. Sing it. Pray it. Enjoy it. Study it with the presence of the Holy Teacher. It will fill you with hope, courage, inspiration, revelation, and joy. **God told Joshua if He would meditate on His Word day and night he would have success.** Even if it's only one verse a day, its honey for your spirit and soul.

- Invite the presence of God into your life through praise— singing about God and to God. Use the Psalms. Get creative! Have fun. Dance around like David did before the Lord. Loosen up. Shake off stress. Thank Him for everything you can think of. Declare who He is: Your Healer, Deliverer, Helper, King, Father, Shepherd who leads you, etc. Praise will transform your thinking. It helps you be aware of Him instead of yourself, your difficulties, and your distractions.

- Talk with (not at) God continually throughout your day. Open the communication line. Practice awareness of Him speaking in many different ways. God wants to hear your words, too, and for you to hear His.

- Go on a "negativity fast" for twenty-one days. Then just do it forever! Practice GRATITUDE instead! Shun negative thoughts, command the demonic powers attached to negativity to go from you. You have authority. Exercise it. Don't let the devil command your thoughts. This is your life, not his to order. Negativity shuts down hearing.

- Forgive other's offenses toward you. This also blocks your hearing—you're too busy rehearsing the offense. It's also an open door for demonic activity in your life; the room gets really crowded when you are listening to their voices, and not God's. If you need to communicate with the offender (or the one you've offended), then call them, write them, text them, whatever—only do it as is appropriate. Ask their forgiveness where you need to and make restitution where you should or can. Unforgiveness will keep you in Bitter Prison—a dark, loveless place. In fact, take a quick check to make sure there isn't an old offense hidden away that needs taking care of. Ask the Holy Spirit to help you.

- Pray in the Spirit—with the spirit of understanding and with the prayer language of the Holy Spirit (tongues). Remember, this is a supernatural life and tongues is a gift from God. You need all the power possible for the battles you face and the new identity you've been given. If you depend solely on your own understanding of how to pray, you're missing the most powerful aspect of prayer—the Spirit who knows *how* to pray! Tongues opens wide the line of communication.

- Get with other believers who are hearing from God. Fellowship creates a synergy of God's presence and nurtures personal growth of your spirit man. It's like receiving rain in your garden. It also brings great encouragement and confirmation of what you are hearing.

These exercises are important. Tend your growth well! You have many enemies that are working around the clock to steal your destiny, identity and maturity. Be militaristic in guarding your heart. It's time to be that warrior bride (of Christ) that Song of Solomon talks about—the sons and daughters who take the Kingdom forcefully, not passively.

These activities will hone your sensitivity to and acquaint you with God's voice. They are like classrooms where we come as humble students hungry to know Him. Daily life is where we work out what He is saying and teaching us, where we cultivate and apply what we hear. Doing so plants the seed deep inside where it can take root and grow, rather than being snatched, scorched or strangled.

# 8

## THE FRUITFUL LIFE: HOLDING ON TO WHAT GOD SAYS

*"And those are the ones on whom seed was sown on the good soil; and they hear the word and accept it and bear fruit, thirty, sixty, and a hundredfold."*
*—Jesus (Mark 4:20)*

Now we come to the second element that the most successful Man said is good soil for growing our valuable identity in Him: **accepting** the word that God speaks to us. Remember, we are creations with free will, and when we hear something from Him, we not only have the grand choice of engaging it, but of holding on to what He says when the going gets tough.

### HEAVEN'S SECRET: GOOD SOIL HOLDS ON TO GOD'S WORDS

In chapter four, we saw how the stony heart joyfully receives what God says, but falls away in difficult times, or when temptation comes. But Jesus doesn't leave us there in the parable, He goes on to show us that the good soil—those with a **good and honest heart**—hold it fast. They accept it and don't let go (Luke 8:15).

To accept God's Word begins with humility. James, the brother of Jesus, instructed the early church to **"humbly accept the Word planted in you"** (James 1:21).

By definition, the word **accept** (Grk: *"paradekhomi"*) means: *"from the hand"*—to readily receive by deliberate intention something that is offered; to make something one's own by taking hold of it and not reject it. To accept a word from God means to receive it, own it, hold on to it, make it yours, don't let go of it—no matter what or who tries to take it away . . . for surely there are many who will try. Circumstances and time itself will try. The whining of the flesh will try. The enemy of your soul for sure will try! Even family, friends, and good Christian church people may try without realizing it.

For "hearing" to become "accepting," it means that desire must deepen into the *devotion* of love—affection that is a divine *determination*. To make a *determination* about something means: a firmness of purpose, will, and intention that does not throw it away when things get challenging. To determine something is to bring it to a conclusion, to settle a matter. No more wishy-washy. No more doubts. No more "hmm, maybe, maybe not". No more abandoning a relationship when something else that looks good comes along. This isn't about striving and self-effort, but is about having the heart of a biblical Daniel who purposed in his heart to stay true to what he heard God speak to him . . . no matter what government, what fire, what lion.

**"My heart is fixed, Oh God, my heart is fixed. . . . One thing have I desired of the Lord and that will I seek after, to behold the beauty of the Lord all the days of my life, and to inquire in His**

temple"—David . . . shepherd, king, father, husband, son, warrior, worshipper (Ps. 57:7; 27:4).

The apostle Paul put it this way: **"Do you not know that those who run in a race all run, but only one receives the prize? Run in such a way that you may win. . . . I press on toward the goal for the prize of the upward call of God in Christ Jesus. . . . Let no one keep defrauding you of your prize (1 Cor. 9:24; Col. 2:18).**

Did you hear that? We can be defrauded of our prize! Tricked. Swindled. Duped. Taken advantage of. Paul said—don't let it happen! Whatever it is, it isn't worth it. . . . Not in comparison to the Prize of Christ.

Circumstances, people, the spirit of the world, and even our own flesh can swindle us from the full maturing of our identity in Christ *if we let them*—if we believe the message they tell us over what God says to us. Our flesh is self-serving and will walk with God as long as everything goes well. It will party in the glory until life comes to a hard place, and then it's hasta luego, arrivadercci, bye-bye. It will bask in the pleasant sun of good times, but it hates the heat of adversity.

Abraham could have let the model of his own father's double-mindedness entice him to settle for less, too. He could have let mental reasoning talk him out of an adventure with God in a strange new place, with apprehension of what he and his family might experience on such a journey. Would they be happy? Safe? What prosperity would they encounter? If any? But he didn't stop short of his call. Not like Adam. Not like Terah. Abraham *owned* the seed of destiny . . . no matter how long the process, the difficulties, the sacrifice. He heard God speak. He took the risk. **He believed in** a divine purpose bigger than himself, reaching further than his own life-time.

It is the same for you and me.

## *OWNING* OUR RELATIONSHIP WITH GOD

Abraham didn't know what was ahead except God's presence. That was sufficient for him. He was a "one thing" man. He saw the goal—the harvest of a life in journey with the Eternal One.

This wasn't sufficient for Terah. Now, you may say that Abraham had a clear word from God, but all Terah had was a gut feeling to move, no clear direct word. You are right. But here is something to consider in this: God will make His desire clear to us as we pay attention to those gut feelings we have from Him. It was Terah's idolatrous heart that kept him from pressing in to know God's full heart in the matter. Thus, he stirred, but then stopped. He didn't move fully with God.

How many times do we stir and then stop? Like one who dreams the dreams of God and awakens, only to return to slumber?

On my own journey, I have had epiphanies of revelation, a quickening from God in my understanding about something, things I was to move forward with, act on, pray through . . . but didn't. I delayed. I lost opportunities, finances, breakthroughs. I had awakened to glimpse something divine, but went back to sleep.

Abraham's embrace of God's plans set in motion a legacy and a lineage that would bless the nations. However, the plan required him to get up and leave everything he'd known—extended family, friends, and a comfortable lifestyle. He no doubt faced people's mockery, misperceptions, and misunderstandings. The plan meant change, and change isn't always easy, especially at Abraham's age. By now, he was over seventy years old and would face many adversities—the greatest perhaps being the years he would wait for the heir that God would promise him. But he held true to his Divine Friend, and the word came to pass.

By now on your journey, you are aware of some things God has spoken to you. You've received them. You've been excited about them, because you have believed them. But now you are in the fire. Going through deep waters. The desert winds are blowing. Time is passing. Finances have dried up. Trouble has visited. Things haven't turned out the way you thought . . . yet, or perhaps not at all. Yet you remember what Father whispered to you. Your heart is struggling to *own* His words, challenged in trusting Him.

It might have been a promise or a command that seemed huge, impossible, maybe even a little unsafe, like stepping out onto water. But you knew it was God . . . but now there has come a challenge. Circumstances have taken you a different way than expected. The test: will you hold on to the word God spoke when adversity knocks? Will you look to *Him* to perform His Word? In the way that He wants to accomplish it? Or will a sandstorm of unbelief bury your seedling?

"Hello. Is this your word?"

"Uhm, it looks like my word. . . . Oh, wait! Let me check my circumstances. Nope. I guess it must have been for someone else."

**Where the heart is not committed to the voice of God, it becomes the fertile ground of denial, rather than destiny.** Judas sold the

Word for money. Eve sold out the Word for earthly wisdom. Adam sold out the Word for a relationship. Terah sold out the awakening of a generational call for the love of other gods. Every human heart has a place of temptation where it can be enticed to sell out. That's why Scripture says the human heart is deceitful above all else. Only love will keep it in the midst of temptation and adversity.

Abraham loved God. He was devoted and committed to his Divine Friend. He heard the Voice, saw destiny, and wouldn't let it go. Besides, what God was asking of him was quite simple, don't you think?—to spend the rest of his life wandering and walking around an unfamiliar region run by godless hostile tribes. I mean, really, how difficult could that be?

## WALKING IN AGREEMENT WITH GOD

God asks, **"How can two walk together unless they agree?"** (Amos 3:3)

As we saw before, our relationship with God is rooted in an everlasting covenant, *an agreement of love,* a union of two, a devotion of hearts. There is nothing more binding than the love between two hearts, even when adversity comes.

**"Many are the afflictions of the righteous, but the Lord delivers him out of them all"** (Ps. 34:19).

Did you hear that? It doesn't say He prevents affliction. Remember, Father isn't raising children with silver spoons in their mouth, but with silver swords in their hands. He's training world rulers. In this world we will have tribulation and affliction, but He's making us as He is: God is love *and* a Mighty Warrior! He is an Overcomer and He is molding our character and nature to resonate with His own. He is forming us as sons and daughters who know how to take authority against destiny stealing demons and delusions of self. And when the heat is on, He doesn't leave us to bake to death, but shades us with the shadow of His wings.

God's love fought for us to the death through Christ on the cross. Is our love for Him as strong? Or do we run at the first arrow of doubt? Is our faith merely religious rhetoric? Or are we truly crucified with the slain Lamb?

Adversity presents defining moments in our life through which we choose to walk humbly with God, snuggle under the shadow of His wings from the searing heat, and send our roots deeper into love's trust and devotion, or not. This may *sound* easy, but the choice isn't always so easy or clear. Sometimes we have to stop and look keenly at where our choice will take us—into God's love and purpose, or away from Him. What is the motive of our choices in moments of adversity?

We can identify with what Adam experienced every time our mind and flesh scream their desires at us. Or like Terah, where our cultural environment lures us to rest in its comfort and compromise. But do we know what it is to be devoted like Abraham, whose love for intimacy with God faced adversity with a relentless hold to the Lover of his soul? Such devotion comes through continual encounters with God that capture the heart's affections. *This* is a work of the Spirit.

**"Blessed is the man who trusts in the Lord, and whose trust is the Lord. For he will be like a tree planted by the water, that**

**extends its roots by a stream, and will not fear when the heat comes; But its leaves will be green, and it will not be anxious in a year of drought, nor cease to yield fruit"**—Jeremiah (Jer. 17:7-8).

Joseph, another example of unyielding faith and undaunting love for God, bore years of unjust imprisonment with humility . . . believing the promise that God gave him in a dream. Now understand this: the trials and difficulties were not his destiny, but each season—regardless of what it seemed—advanced him toward a full harvest in his life as he held to the word of the Lord. He kept his heart free of offense in the process. He had a call to be a great leader, but he understood that his heart had to be in the right place for what he saw as his identity in covenant with God.

Joseph's dream was not about people bowing to him as to a tyrant ruler, but he saw himself as a righteous son positioned with God-given authority for a divine purpose.

**"They afflicted his [Joseph's] feet with fetters, he himself was laid in irons; until the time that his word came to pass, the word of the Lord tested him"** (Ps. 105:18-19, clarification mine).

Hearing God's voice and seeing our identity in a love relationship with Him is the superglue that holds our heart to His through thick and thin, for better or for worse, in sickness and in health. It makes us not faint in the day of adversity. It makes our strength great, and not small.

**The devotion of LOVE is a commitment to the one it loves.** This is a love that comes from the Holy Spirit. Such love creates a buoyant spirit, an unquenchable passion, a root that runs deep. It has ears that hear and eyes that look for the glory of the Lord, and will not settle for less. Here we become enamored, not with self-exaltation, but with the fragrance of His presence who is the Rose of Sharon and Lily of the Valley. Our heart, like that of a bride, has determined—has settled the matter once and for all—we want no other.

It is not enough to receive the "engagement ring of salvation" that gives us entrance to heaven. We want to slip on the marriage ring with a heart that forsakes every other love to have just one . . . just Him . . . no matter what, forever. We listen to His words because we love Him, and we hold on to what He says, believing He is true, because we love Him . . . because He loves us. And He *is* true—He is not a liar.

**"Teacher, what is the great commandment in the law? And He said to him, 'You shall love the Lord your God with all your heart, and with all your soul, and with all your mind'"** –Jesus (Matt. 22:36-37).

## STAYING TRUE THROUGH ADVERSITY

Scripture is full of those who stayed true to God in adversity: Abraham, Daniel and his three friends, Paul, and others as well who left homes, who served God in the midst of pagan cultures, passed through fire rather than worshipping idols, faced lions, endured stoning, shipwreck, and imprisonment all because of their devotion to the Holy One. And the greatest of all is Jesus, who left His home in glory to be born a baby, who walked faithfully with God, and humbled himself to the death of the cross, rose again and returned to the Father. *His* devotion to love the Father with all the heart, soul, mind, and strength is what the Holy Spirit pours into our hearts, too. We couldn't do this without God—without the work of the Spirit and the Son, and the Father who sent them!

Hebrews 11 gives us a long list of those who held on, stood firm, refused to give up, held confident in God in spite of the fact that they had to wait, wandered as strangers, faced the impossible, or were "sawn in two". Ouch! These all depended upon the Divine One to perform what they could not. They withstood the tempest, because they were rooted in Love.

Fox's Book of Martyrs has recorded testimonies of those killed for Christ throughout the centuries. It describes how many **sang** as they were being tortured, burned, or beheaded . . . and how loved ones watched as family members and friends perished by the cruel hands of persecutors. How on earth could people sing in the face of death, in pain? It is said that they were more conscious of the reality of Him than the pain in their heart or body. They stood faithfully by God, like Abraham with his Divine Friend.

**"Though He slay me, I will hope in Him"**—Job (Job 13:15).

*"Hope"* (Grk. *"elpis"*)—the joyful expectation of good.

Hope sees beyond a point of death. It sees resurrection. It sees reward. The martyrs saw beyond death and rejoiced. They saw glory. They saw a harvest that would come of their faithfulness. They saw fruitfulness for Father.

**"Let us not lose heart in doing good, for in due time we will reap if we do not grow weary"** (Gal. 6:9).

Sometimes we must look beyond death—beyond a relationship, a career, a position, a painful circumstance, a loss, to see the **harvest**

**of possibilities** that God can create out of anything. Out of all things. Out of nothing. Father wants us to dare to lift our eyes and see the One who works all things together for good for those who love Him and are called according to His purpose (Rom. 8:28).

The One who turns our mourning into dancing.

The One who removes our funeral clothes and dresses us with gladness.

**"With people this is impossible, but with God all things are possible"**—Jesus (Matt. 19:26).

Why does God allow adversity? Why do some seem to be kissed with favor among men, and others kissed with betrayals? I don't know the full answer to every situation, but I do know this—a defining, refining, and a shift takes place inside us during adversity. We either resolve to reach toward God and dig our roots deeper into Him, or we turn away to go deeper into self. Our focus either resolves to magnify God, or magnify our circumstance above Him. In adversity we make choices—to commit our way to God, or make our own way.

Nevertheless, even when we fail: **"Faithful is He who calls you, and He also will bring it to pass"** (1 Thess. 5:24).

## THE WORK OF GOD IN ADVERSITY

Years ago, the Lord called our family to move to Dallas, Texas. The move was going great—someone purchased our house with all cash, my husband's job transferred him, a great rental home opened up right away, and the ball was rolling for working with a new ministry in the Dallas area with some close friends of ours.

The night before our move, a situation transpired that kicked off a season of adversity and testing that lasted nearly five years. It was a season of fire. We could have walked away from a difficult situation at any time, but one thing held us steady—we knew that God had ordained our steps. We held on to His Word and waited on Him. And as David said, **"He brought me out into a spacious place; He rescued me because He delighted in me"** (Ps. 18:19 NIV).

God used that time to do a work in me, working all things together for good. Later He connected us with another ministry, under which I can truly say, I met destiny. He positioned us to be in the right place at the right time . . . though the way there was not always a comfortable ride!

The fire of adversity brings up the truth of our motives and ambitions. It gets to the *heart* of the matter. Adversity tests our love and willingness to truly follow Christ, following the Lamb wherever He goes—not just to mountain tops of glory, but to the cross. It gets to the bottom-line of who we are, our character, our responses, where we put our trust, and what is really important to us.

Adversity has a unique effect upon the heart that either deepens our desire to be conformed to Christ's image—laying down our life and allowing the work of the Spirit to cleanse us—or we turn away and love grows cold. It will test the reality of our confession of being buried with Christ and risen in new life. It will test our vision: can we see beyond the grave? Can we see the harvest that will bless many if we cultivate faithfulness to what God is saying to us? Can we dare love and trust God in our circumstances? Will we draw our comfort from the Comforter, or from the world?

Can we see the fruit that comes of faithfulness?

King David begins writing the 93rd Psalm with an encouragement to not fret, stew, or be envious of others' gain. He said, **"Trust in the Lord and do good; dwell in the land and cultivate faithfulness"** (Ps. 37:3). He continues to edify the hearer with: **"delight yourself in God . . . commit your way to Him."** He knew that faithfulness has great reward.

**"Unless a grain of wheat falls into the earth and die, it remains alone; but if it dies, it bears much fruit"**—Jesus (John 12:24).

## WHEN HOLDING ON MEANS LETTING GO

Sometimes holding on to what God says also means letting go— letting go of offenses, resentment, selfish ambition, personal agendas, and unforgiveness toward the one who has been the instrument of our adversity: who threw us in a pit, stripped our goods, removed favor, betrayed us, bruised us, left us for dead. Joseph forgave his brothers who sold him as a slave, an action that thrust him onto a path of *seemingly* wasted years and lost destiny. But they weren't wasted years. They were useful training years for Joseph's identity *because he committed them to His loving Creator who had a good plan for him.* Just like those years of adversity I experienced, they were not wasted years. They were useful learning times.

**"And we know that God causes all things to work together for good to those who love God, to those who are called according to His purpose"** (Rom. 8:28).

Joseph held on *and* let go. Doing so enabled him to not drag yesterday's wounds into present promotions.

Sometimes it's our control and anger toward God that we must let go—anger when we feel that He doesn't seem to be particularly moved by our affliction—anger that He lets bad things happen to good people. To us. To loved ones. Anger that we serve Him and yet He lets us experience pain, loss, or devastation. But God *is* moved by our affliction. He also knows the battle that wages against us, our heart, and our faith. He also sees the harvest that will come of our faith that looks to Him in times of adversity, when we are tested by fire.

**"Put me like a seal over your heart, like a seal on your arm, for love is as strong as death"** (Song of Sol. 8:6).

## LOVE THAT "TAKES HEART" IN ADVERSITY

Our engagement with God's love and voice is what will give us wings to rise above our circumstance and soar with His perspective. But what do we do when we can't feel God, see Him, or sense His love and nearness? So often in times of adversity, that is what we feel . . . like God has left the premises. But He hasn't. He's right there. If we will continue to look to Him, the Comforter *will* help us to stand back up when we've been knocked for a hard loop. He will restore our heart as He pours grace and love into it—love that empowers us with authority over the darkness that affliction brings to our mind.

Jesus endured suffering because He trusted His Father, received the comfort of the Spirit, and because He saw beyond the grave— He saw us. Can we see Him in our moment of affliction? Can we see past this moment? Sometimes we can't. But He sees, and His love never lets us go.

"Therefore we do not lose heart, but though our outer man is decaying, yet our inner man is being renewed day by day. For momentary, light affliction is producing for us an eternal weight of glory far beyond all comparison, while we look not at the things which are seen, but at the things which are not seen; for the things which are seen are temporal, but the things which are not seen are eternal"—Paul (2 Cor. 4:16-18).

Paul said that God's grace is sufficient for *whatever* we go through—a grace that makes us strong, even in our weakness. The Comforter is the Spirit of Grace whose influence upon our heart enables us to *stand firm* and *rejoice in hope*! So here's the question: what influence are we listening to in times of distress? Is it, "Let me outta here!"?

Paul, well acquainted with adversities, said that we *"glory"* in adversity and tribulation, knowing that it works *patience* in us— you know, the "p" word. Patience gives us the experience that life isn't all about us, and that God *will* bring us through. While our expectation in people often fails, expectation in God never fails because God is unceasingly faithful and what He says is true. And He proves Himself in this matter time and time again. Therefore, we can have a joyful expectation that good *is* coming our way!

"Love bears all things, believes all things, hopes all things, endures all things" (1 Cor. 13:7).

Meanwhile, cultivate faithfulness and good will come.

## SINGING IN THE RAIN

Are you tempted to give up? Stop short? Sit on the ground with ashes on your head? (O.T. ritual for sorrow). Do you feel dirt-desert-dry? Is your soul sick of waiting for some promise? Has Prosperity left the premise? Here's what the Holy Spirit says—**Rejoice! Even though you're being distressed by various trials, for these are the refining fires that purifies the gold of faith within you. Sing and make melody with your heart to the Lord. Give thanks in everything!** (1 Pet. 1:6-7; Eph. 5:19 paraphrase mine)

Ughh. But I don't feel like singing. My throat is too parched. My eyes are too weary with crying, and I can't see the words on the hymn sheet. My mind is too tired to think with all this heat and my heart is too heavy to eek out a note. And I'm mad. Disappointed. Deeply. Let someone else sing.

Someone else is.

The Father, Son, and Holy Spirit are singing over you. God, who is the Creator of Light melody and healing harmony, the great Composer of spiritual song and Heavenly Conductor of renewed soul sound, sings over you. He knows that dry ground is death to a seed, and so He sings songs of deliverance over you to keep the seed of who you are alive in the midst of your drought. He wants you to join Him in His song.

**"You are my hiding place; You preserve me from trouble; You surround me with songs of deliverance. Selah [stop and think about that!]"** (Psalm 32:7 clarification mine).

He surrounds us with songs in the day and gives us songs in the night. Pay attention to the song that may awaken you in the morning. No, not the radio. The song in your spirit, your heart, or simply your thoughts. It may be Him singing. He loves to sing, you know. He loves to sing over you! **"The Lord your God in the midst of you is mighty; He will save, He will rejoice over you with joy. He will rest in His love, He will joy over you with singing"** (Zeph. 3:17).

And what's more, His song can come through any means. A friend of mine told me the other day how she was recently watching a television show, and when one of the singers sang, it was as if God was singing the words to her, telling her how beautiful she is to Him. She suddenly felt overwhelmed with God's love. God loves to burst into our life with the revelation of His heart toward us through any means! He uses the simplest ways to draw us into experience with Him.

Music has a powerful influence upon a seed. Even science has discovered this fact and effect. Melodic sound waves, like water, have the ability to awaken a dormant seed, ignite its germination, and encourage its growth at the cellular level. It has been found that fire also has the propensity to awaken a dormant seed.

How much more then does the water and fire of God's voice, the song of the Creator, our Father, have influence upon our whole being—spirit, soul, and body—awakening and strengthening the movement of the seed of identity within us. When God sings, something happens inside us. **We begin to resonate with the sound of His heart and His words rather than the difficulty of our circumstances.** That song of His presence is like rain to our spirit, soul, and mind. It is water for the seed of His Word within us.

A heart filled with the song of God is like a garden with fresh rain.

As we hear His song over us and agree with His melody, our spirit, thoughts, and emotions will begin to move simultaneously on the same wave length of His faith, hope, and joy. Just as natural music influences mood (creating both stimulating and soothing influence on our mental and emotional state), so *spiritual song* refreshes new resolve in our spirit, renews our mind, and puts a dance of victory in our feet, when just a moment ago our feet were "in the stocks". It fans the flame of persevering love that believes the vision we saw. It refocuses our perspective and reminds us of truth that we may have momentarily forgotten in the "heat of the moment". It awakens the anointing within us to take authority in our circumstances.

**"And the Lord will continually guide you, and satisfy your desire in scorched places, and give strength to your bones; and you will be like a watered garden, and like a spring of water whose waters do not fail"** (Isa. 58:11).

Even the world recognizes the powerful dynamic of music to move and inspire the heart. Did you know that the very cells of our body carry melody? The core of our cells is light (energy), and moving energy has sound. Just as negative thoughts deplete us of life-giving energy, the song of the Lord returns the glimmer in our eye, and spark in our soul. **It quickens our hands to pick up the weapons of our spiritual warfare and wage a victorious engagement in the battle we face.**

## Praise Changes Our Atmosphere

No wonder God tells us **one hundred and twenty times** in His Word to sing praise to Him. **Praise changes the atmosphere around us as it changes the atmosphere within us.** God's presence rests on the praises of His people. Our melodic declaration of faith draws His manifest presence to us. Praise is a horn of power when adversity comes, because it summons the help of God while putting gladness in our heart. And merriness makes us feel great! The enemy doesn't want us happy or healthy. He wants us grumbling with ingratitude, sick with sorrow, heavy with heartache, dizzy with disappointment, moaning a dirge, a lament, a sad song.

Without a doubt, every one of us has lost our song at one time or another. We may not have realized it, but it is felt as a depletion of heart motivation. But we were created to sing, whether we have a natural talent for it or not. An internal song is part of our DNA: spirit, soul, and body. I remember going through another season—one of disappointment and failed expectations one after the other. I didn't realize how it was affecting me until one day I recognized a pattern forming: decreased prayer and boredom with worship services. And that just wasn't me!

Then one evening at church, as I sat watching the musicians play and the congregation engage the presence of God, I suddenly became aware of how disconnected I was . . . and had been for some time. I thought, *Oh God, I've lost my song!*—not the melody in my mouth, but the tune in my heart. Once I recognized it, I asked God, *why*. And He answered me. Then began my song-recovery process as He got to the root of my disappointments and issues with Him and my circumstances. Yes, sometimes we have issues with God!

We are the offspring of the Lion of *Judah*. Judah means *"Praise!"* Praise is our trumpet, our roar, against the seed scorcher: "You shall not have the harvest that glorifies my Father!" What's more, praise is a great digger-outer of stones in the heart. Try praising and staying angry or bitter. You can't! Why? Because praise invites the presence of God and when He comes, honey, you can't stay in your pity-party or pride. His presence is a fire that doesn't scorch the seed, but purifies the soil as it brings out the dross and impurities in us so He can remove them from us.

Praise is a *favorable environment* to the seed of who we are in Christ. It softens any hardness and nurtures our faith to wait on God as we declare His goodness. Praise fans the flame of love in the heart. It is the breath that fills our spiritual lungs when passing through breath-taking circumstances.

**"Let everything that has breath praise the Lord. . . . Oh that men would praise the Lord!"** (Ps. 150:6; 107:8)

## THE POWER OF GOD IN YOU

If you have lost your song in the midst of adversity, then the Lord wants to restore it right now. Paul said that you have a treasure from God—an internal, abiding power from God, and not of yourself. His keeping power surrounds you in the midst of affliction so that you are not crushed, though you may sometimes feel like it; not despairing even though you may feel perplexed; not forsaken though you may be facing persecution; and not destroyed even though you may have been struck down by some cruel blow.

The treasure we carry within us is both the power of the cross and the power of His resurrection (2 Cor. 4:7-10).

**"Finally, be strong in the Lord and in the strength of His might. Put on the full armor of God, so that you will be able to stand firm against the schemes of the devil. For our struggle is not against fles h and blood, but against the rulers, against the powers, against the world forces of this darkness of this age, against the spiritual forces of wickedness in the heavenly places. Therefore, take up the full armor of God so that you will be able to resist in the evil day, and having done everything, to stand firm"** (Eph. 6:10-13).

I pray that the encouragement of the Lord cover you right now, in whatever situation you find yourself. May He pour fresh vision into every area of discouragement, and courage where you have despaired. You have a destiny to fulfill. Keep going. Hold on to what God has spoken to you, no matter what. He is faithful. Get your heart into the place of agreement with Him. Remember, the spirit of the world has one intention—to destroy the holy seed within you. But Father has another plan—to make you fruitful through renewed intimacy with Him.

## LAB CLASS: HOLDING ON TO WHAT GOD SAYS

What adversity is facing the word that God has given you right now? What do you need to resolve in your heart regarding what God has spoken? What steps do you need to take to  continue building the seed of destiny within you? Here are some steps to help practice accepting with joy what God says.

- Take the list that you wrote of what God has said to you (from our last chapter) and write what obstacles have come against those words. Then ask Him for His counsel on how to overcome those obstacles. Write them down. Example:

**Word Spoken:** _____

**Challenge:** _____

**Counsel of God:** _____

- Identify areas of grief and disappointment. Allow yourself to feel the anger, pain, and loss, like David did. Recognize their reality and the internal messages they give you, then feel and declare what God says. Example:

**ADVERSITY**
A parent's rejection

**HOW I FEEL**
Hurt

**INTERNAL MESSAGE**
I am unloved

**WHAT GOD SAYS**
I am eternally loved!

- Practice forgiveness—identify the grudges and let them go.

**OFFENSE**
Mistreated

**HOW I FEEL**
Demeaned

**INTERNAL MESSAGE**
I'm worthless

**WHAT GOD SAYS**
Forgive them / I'm greatly valued!

- Practice praying for those who are the instruments of adversity in your life. Bless them. Ask Father to help you see them as He sees them.

- Practice listening for God's song over you. Put on some worship music and get into the presence of God. Ask Him to help you hear His song. Soak in the Light. Ask Him to help you to hear Him as you sleep at night and when you wake.

- Practice praising! Praise Him for His goodness and provision. Sing from your heart. Incorporate clapping and even the dance—dance over the darkness, scattering its presence from your life. Use an instrument if you play one as you release your song.
  - Praise changes the atmosphere from earthly to divine

- Praise brings single-minded focus on God and His ability
- Praise is the gateway of revelation and wisdom from God
- Praise develops spiritual eyes and ears
- Praise develops humility
- Praise clothes us with God's beauty and His armor
- Praise changes our perspective from a servant to a son
- Praise releases prophecy
- Praise is a bearer of good news that encourages the heart
- Praise invites the presence of God
- Praise is the acceptable offering of love

# 9

## THE FRUITFUL LIFE: BEARING FRUIT WITH PERSEVERANCE

*"And those are the ones on whom seed was sown on the good soil;and they hear the word and accept it and bear fruit, thirty, sixty, and a hundredfold."*
*—Jesus (Mark 4:20)*

Here we are now, at the point where the word we've received blossoms with fruit. Finally! We've seen the miraculous journey of hearing God and accepting what He says, but we've got one more important element needed to succeed in bringing *all* the seed God gives us to full harvest. That is, *bearing* His words with perseverance for multiplication.

Different seed in differing times and locations will render varying degrees of fruitfulness—sometimes thirtyfold, sixtyfold, or even a hundred times over. God may have us labor with something He has spoken to us about for a time, and then focus on cultivating another word in a new season. Each seed that we faithfully cultivate *will* be fruitful, but each may have different crop abundance.

What this means for us is, our job is never done! No retirement in God. No kicking off our shoes and lying on the couch, letting the "good times roll" because we've done our part. He labors, we labor! There is more seed to grow and new fruit to be had in each new season of our life. And even the first word He spoke to us will continue to render more fruit as we follow His guidance in gardening and persevering.

### HEAVEN'S SECRET: GOOD SOIL IS ABIDING LOVE THAT PERSEVERES

In Luke 8:15, this "bearing fruit" of varying degrees of harvest is described as being accomplished with *perseverance*—carrying and supporting a life as with a pregnant woman, or like a parent with a beloved child until it is fully developed in every way. Continued "parenting" of the seeds that God gives us **(yes, God will give us many seeds to nurture)** requires persevering, not just through adversity, but through the passing years. And what is the power of this perseverance? Of not tiring out or losing focus? The key is *abiding love.*

Abiding love is the fire of relentless love that grows brighter, not dimmer. A love that doesn't wane in the midst of a world where passion falls prey to passivity, complacency, and compromise. Remember, children are the *produce* of love—that's why we call it *reproduction!* They are produced through love and must be nurtured to fullness through love. God lovingly parents us, and we must do the same with the seed He gives us—our gifts, talents, character, and intimacy with Him—that produces fruit to nurture His harvest in others.

**"But the path of the righteous is like the light of dawn that shines brighter and brighter until the full day"**— Solomon (Prov. 4:18).

**"As for you, let that abide in you which you heard from the beginning. If what you heard from the beginning abides in you, you also will abide in the Son and in the Father. . . . I am the Vine, you are the branches; he who abides in Me and I in him, he bears much fruit, for apart from Me you can do nothing. . . . My Father is glorified by this, that you bear much fruit, and so prove to be My disciples."** (I John 2:24; John 15:5)

**"Keep yourselves in the love of God . . ."** —Jude (Jude 1:21).

Keeping is an active choice. Love is an active choice.

In Matthew 13:23, Jesus said it is the *"man"* or *"person"* who bears the fruit, not God. *We* have the grand task, no—privilege and delight—of engaging with God to bear His fruit in our life. A branch will bear fruit as long as it's healthy and continues to drink from the vine. It will have new fruit in each new season. This natural picture shows us that our health and fruitfulness requires *consistent unity with God and intimacy with Him.* He is the Author of our life and Divine Lover of our soul, and this relationship is what creates an ecosystem appropriate for the success of our full harvest.

Remember, fruit isn't for our benefit, but for others. The earth is hungry for the fruit of God through you and me. It is being fed a diet of darkness and death by the god of this world—served from a menu of fear, hatred, and selfishness; it is waiting, desperate, for the fruit of light through you and me. It's waiting for heaven's provision to be opened through an access that we carry with us wherever we go, an access to which we've been given the keys.

We live in a world surrounded by forces, both within and without, that want to destroy our intimacy with God—our hearing His voice, our accepting what He says, and our abiding in Him. Those powers want to shut down our heavenly access by enticing our flesh (that listens!) lest we flourish with Kingdom purpose. Satan is the father of such forces and an independent spirit that does not abide in God. This independent, self-exalting nature is the message he touted in heaven to deceive a third of the angels who were then cast out of heaven with him. It's the same message he brought to earth in the Garden of Eden. So attractive. So deadly. The killer of abiding love.

It is the same message he tries to bring to our garden to cut off our success as God's children, to cut off fruitful love.

Every place in the earth where God says, "This place is Mine," Satan seeks to establish a *denial of God*. In Eden he entered as a snake saying, "Did God really say?" In the ancient Jerusalem temple it was idols brought into the Holy Place to defile the worship of the Holy One. On the current temple mount, it is a house of worship that *denies the Son*. And in our heart, it is the things of the world—its lusts, cares, and passivity toward Jesus—that Satan wants to sow.

There is an old hymn whose words, penned by Robert Robinson, reflect the heart's weakness to wander and be independent of God . . . words that I can identify with on my own human journey with the Holy Spirit who is teaching me to abide in God's love, lest I drift, become passive, and thus, powerless. Look at the last stanza of this beautiful song, *Come Thou Fount*:

*"O to grace how great a debtor, daily I'm constrained to be!*
*Let Thy goodness, like a fetter, bind my wandering heart to Thee;*
*Prone to wander, Lord, I feel it, prone to leave the God I love;*
*Here's my heart, O take and seal it; seal it for Thy courts above. A-men."*

Robert understood the heart's need to be "sealed" as God's dwelling place. *Sealed* means: to have a tight closure so that nothing enters to corrupt. In this case, what corrupts is the voice of another that would woo the heart away from God. What voice? The echo of our flesh and the spirit of the world who, like lovers, gleefully hold hands and run off to romp in folly, a folly of apathy toward God.

**"Do not love the world nor the things in the world. If anyone loves the world, the love of the Father is not in him"** (1 John 2:15).

We've all known a love for God that is prone to wander: intimacy with God that falters, faith that stalls in its growth, and busyness that replaces fruitfulness (yes, we can be busy and not fruitful). We get distracted. We strive. Our gifts and talents wane in purity and power as they engage an agenda for *our* purposes rather than God's. We are all familiar with a love that doesn't abide, remain, or persevere.

In our American culture, we know a lot about love that *doesn't* last— where lovers don't commit to one another. Where eyes drift and hands let go. Where love is self-serving and is just "for the moment," a one-night stand. Where selfish desires enter the back door causing the spouse to leave the front one. Where lovers move on, or become unloving, perhaps even harmful, and the tie must be broken for the sake of safety. Close friends betray and desert us.

Recently, as I was going home from work, I heard on the radio this

171

news broadcast: "Many Americans are now finding that marriage is no longer necessary." What? Oh, my gosh! It was so out-there, reported so matter-of-fact, so no-big-deal as the commentator moved on to other news. The (horrifying) announcement of the family nuclear explosion passed in less than a blink. Not even a "that's too bad." The reality that the broadcaster was so nonchalantly stating was: the commitment to a journey of love with one person is no longer needed or desired by a growing number in our society. We can love and leave at convenience.

In other words, abiding love is no longer necessary.

This is contrary to the heart of God whose very nature is commitment to relationship! He Himself is an eternal unity of Three as One! Faithful hearts in a marriage union, or even friendship, is a reflection of the heart of God—a reflection of heaven on earth. This is not a condemnation to anyone who has gone through a divorce, as I realize that some cannot continue in a marriage because of abuse, repeated unfaithfulness, and circumstances beyond their control. We live in a world where relationships are often full of unrelenting thorns too poisonous to work through. And for some, the choice was not theirs, but one imposed by a false lover.

God's love is neither harmful nor wanes. It is for a life time . . . and beyond. His love is faithful and His mercies are new every morning. The very act of infidelity was the heart-rending grief that God felt, and wrote about in the Old Testament, regarding His people who pursued the love of other gods. Just like Terah, who knew truth, but was swayed by a culture that worshipped other gods.

Is this not also the heartache and indictment that Jesus spoke of in the book of Revelation? **"I know your works, and labor, and patience . . . but I have somewhat against you because you have left your first love"** (Rev. 2:2-4). How vulnerable is the human heart to wander from the love of God! Jesus had the same issue with the religious leaders of His day when He said, **"But I know you, that you do not have the love of God in yourselves"** (John 5:42). They had the Temple and the Torah, but no glory in the Holy of Holies. No intimacy with God in the heart. **But intimacy with God, His voice, and His glory are what shapes and forms the very core of who we are as His children!**

God says that He created us to be a "holy people"—lives and hearts set apart for Him in a world where other gardens are entertaining the devil's words. A world where idols are brought into their inner sanctuary, and whose worship denies the Son (thus denies the work of the cross and resurrection by the Spirit).

"Hey, Mac. Give me another scotch on the rocks."

"It's your fifth one, Joe. You've got someone to drive you home?"

"Yeah, yeah, yeah. Julie will be here soon. We've got Bible study to go to this evening."

The word "love" that Jesus used in Rev. 2:2-4, is *"agape"*. Agape means: *divine affection; a love feast.* According to Jesus, His Church was doing "good" things, but their heart's affection had left the banquet table of His love. They loved the works of their hands more than intimacy with Him. Does that sound familiar to you? It does to me . . . prone to wander, Lord, I feel it! We can do this with anything in life, including ministry without even realizing it.

We can be so busy doing "God's work" that we forget about Him. We can get so wrapped up in doing what He said that we neglect time in His presence, putting everything aside to be with Him. Even as I've been writing this book, in the midst of time constraints with a job and other responsibilities, I've had to remind myself not to let a "good work" pre-empt intimate time with God. It's easy to get up first thing in the morning and flip open my computer instead of my Bible. But the word He speaks of what we are to *do*, must never supersede who we *are* with Him.

True love is a commitment to the loved one. God is committed to us. Are we committed to Him? Are we *set apart* for Him in our thinking and choices? Do we love Him with all our heart, soul, mind, and strength? Is the love in our relationship with Him fresh? Does the fire of love for Him persevere through the seasons and years without waning?

## RETURN TO EDEN

**Abiding love is the energizing flow by which His Word in us, and our identity in Him, will come to full and multiplied fruition.** It is a current of delight with our Heavenly Friend, like Abraham experienced. The deepest well of any good lasting marriage or friendship is the refreshing waters of delight. The bride in Song of Solomon 5:16 says, **"His mouth is full of sweetness. And he is wholly desirable. This is my beloved and this is my friend, O daughters of Jerusalem."** She sounds pretty delighted with him, doesn't she?

This is so different from the picture we see in James 4:4 of *believers* whose delight was in the world and its lusts, rather than the love of God. James defined it as spiritual adultery. He said that the friendship with the (spirit of the) world makes us *enemies* of God! Why? Because God is a jealous God and He doesn't want our heart divided with another. Mr. Spirit of the World is an intruder in the heart of Christ's Bride. Believe me, he will steal our harvest.

How do you see Jesus? As the *desire* and *delight* of your life? It's okay to be honest.

Delight is a key element of love that lasts. Delight perpetuates momentum in *any* relationship and keeps it moving forward. God delights in us, and to be with us. He delights in giving us keys to overcome and rule in life, and to see us prosper. He delights to supernaturally work with us for full success in who He created us to be in Him (Prov. 8:31; Ps. 35:27).

King David lived his life in the delight of God. Listen to how he described people in relationship with God: **"They drink their fill in the abundance of Your house; and You give them to drink of the river of Your delights"** (Ps. 36:8). Now listen to this! The word *"delights"* here in Hebrew is *"eden"*. Yes, you got it! It is the same word used in Genesis as the Garden of Eden. It means: luxury, finery, delights, pleasure. "House" speaks of intimacy and family, and also referred to the temple, the place of God's dwelling. The word "river" means: torrents. In other words, we experience an overwhelming flow of abundance and delight in the place where God dwells.

*Eden* (delight) is where Adam and Eve were told to be fruitful children exercising dominion over the earth. Now, that garden of delight—*Eden*— is in us! That's right, folks. It's not in Mesopotamia

175

any more. And God's glory doesn't shine from the ancient Tabernacle in the wilderness anymore either. The place of divine communion and delight in His glory is right inside us—inside the tabernacle of the garden-heart.

His presence is the place of true success. This is where we prosper.

This is where our gifts and talents prosper in the work and labor we are called to do.

This is where we carry the seed of His Word and our identity in Him to full fruition and multiplication, because it's the place where our heart communes with His.

King Solomon was raised in the faith of his father, King David. His divinely inspired book—the Song of Solomon—is a beautiful picture and allegory of the loving relationship between Christ and His Bride (the believer). He paints the heart of the Bridal Believer as being like a garden set apart with choice fruits for her Beloved Christ—a garden "enclosed" meaning that she has boundaries with what should, and shouldn't, be there. Her heart is designed for her Beloved and no other. She says His kisses are better than wine and speaks of Him as the "one whom her soul loves." She isn't satisfied with another's attention or affection. She wants Him. Nothing else compares to His love and the delight of His friendship.

When Jesus walks into our garden-heart, what does He find? Someone waiting for Him? Or hiding from Him? Does He find Mr. Cares molesting our heart? Does He discover our affections entwined in the arms of Mr. Wealth? Does He enter and see Mr. Worldly Pleasure ravaging us with kisses? Or does He see one whose heart is totally His?

Do you find the kiss of intimacy with Christ better than your lips on a drink? Better than your favorite T.V. show? Better than the affirmation from your career? Better than the bed of someone who isn't your spouse? Do you see Him as the One whom your soul loves most? Do you see your life and gifts fruitful for Him?

**"How blessed is the man who does not walk in the counsel of the wicked, nor stand in the path of sinners, nor sit in the seat of scoffers! But his delight is in the law [Torah] of the LORD, and in His law he meditates day and night. He will be like a tree firmly planted by streams of water, which yields its fruit in its season, and its leaf does not wither; and in whatever he does, he prospers"** (Ps.1:1-3 – emphasis mine).

The word *"delight"* here is (Heb.) *"chephet"* and means: "to affect with great pleasure, the gratification of senses and the mind." Did you notice what special delight the psalmist said makes a person fruitful and prosperous? The "Torah" of God! The voice of God! The Torah is the instruction, directives, and body of prophetic teaching of God. David (the psalmist here) meditated in it day and night. He gave God his full attention because the delight of Him filled his senses, thoughts, and heart with great pleasure!

Does the delight of God fill your senses? Does the delight of God fill your gifts and talents? Or are worldly pleasures dulling your sense of God, creating passivity and apathy in your relationship with Him? Stealing your choice fruit for Him and giving it to the spirit of the world. The garden of God that is mixed with the world kills the choice fruits of harvest intended for the Beloved.

**"Oh, taste and see that the Lord is good"** (Psalm 34:8a).

## THE NURTURING ENERGY OF DELIGHT

In the movie, *Chariots of Fire*, Eric Liddell said, "I feel His pleasure when I run". We were created for God's pleasure, to experience pleasure! Our gifts and talents in sync with His voice is designed to elicit a delightful resonation inside us. It makes us want to be even more fruitful in how He made us! **Growing in our spiritual and natural identity was always intended to be a satisfying experience.**

God's purpose is that we delight in the things He gives us. Not apart from Him, but with Him, satisfying Him *and* us with Kingdom fruitfulness. Every parent's delight is to see their child prosper and happy. And the truth is, we won't stay around, or do something for very long, if we don't enjoy it. The great thing about Heaven's success, spiritually and naturally, is that we get to cultivate something we enjoy as we develop how we are made for the benefit of another, with the presence of God!

Delight is the energy that keeps a couple together: sharing dreams, building with like-minded vision, experiencing joy together, and affirming one another. Love that lasts gives attention to the other. It makes the other feel like they matter, like they are special. God certainly makes us feel like we matter. He couldn't have done any more than what He did through His Son on the cross.

How do we make God feel in our life? Do we make Him feel like He is our greatest treasure? Valued? Like He matters most to us? Or a close second? Love in any relationship doesn't die without a reason—it dies from neglect and lack of attention. It dies when delight isn't nurtured through joyful experience.

Abraham didn't have a church family, or the written Torah (Scripture) to read in his day. He didn't have worship concerts, Christian CDs, inspirational self-help books, prophetic conferences, or the myriad things we have to nurture our walk with God. What he *did* have was the presence of God and the voice of God. And God shared with him about His dream of a city that He was building—a people living in passionate relationship with Him . . . a Bride, a New Jerusalem.

I think Abraham must have listened on the edge of his seat to the stories of his forefathers who knew God, who recounted to him the ways and acts of the Divine Presence. We do not know where Noah and Shem lived in proximity to Abraham when he was growing up, but we do know from chronological passages that they were still alive at the time Abraham was born, and that family clans often held tightly together. How important our testimonies are to inspire others regarding the truth and goodness of God, and the experiences we've had with Him. God tells us to share our testimonies from generation to generation.

God intends for our spiritual experience with Him and His Kingdom to be our daily "norm"—just as natural as how we experience this world with our natural senses. He wants us more aware of His presence than we are of another in the room; where His world is more real than this one; where the pictures and words I perceive in my spirit are more valid than what my physical eyes see and ears hear around me. Such engagement with the dimension of God's world nurtures who I am as His child. It is the engagement with Father's world that grows and matures me as a child of Light.

As I drink of His Word, resonate with His voice, feel His touch, and experience His world—these develop the understanding of my identity in Him.

And what else is produced by this delightful engagement with God's love and friendship? Laughter! We see this with Abraham, God's Friend, at the birth of his son, Isaac. Isaac was a long waited for promise from God, and Isaac's name means *"laughter"*!

## THE NURTURING ENVIRONMENT OF JOY

**"These things I have spoken to you so that My joy may be in you, and that your joy may be made full"**—Jesus (John 15:11).

The abiding love of God fills us with joy. Joy is a fundamental *dynamic* of the Kingdom of God. Webster's Dictionary describes "dynamic" *as an energy that produces undergoing change and development, a force that produces motion.* Joy is more than a happy attitude. It is the oxygen of God's presence, the energy of the Spirit that develops us, changes us, produces internal growth, and generates momentum in God, with our gifts and talents, in relationships, with vision. Joy is a critical element of good soil!

*"In Your presence is fullness of joy; in Your right hand there are pleasures forever"*—King David (Ps. 16:11b). You know, it's not just the world that has pleasures—the pleasures in His presence FAR outweigh earthly pleasures! His right hand speaks of strength and power. Jesus is called the Right Hand of God. The presence of Jesus releases joy that strengthens, empowers, and heals.

Did you know that "joy" is referenced 180 times in Scripture? Joy is a big deal to God! Doubt and fear make us sad and powerless, but God's presence that is full of joy makes us *feel* like we can do all things through Christ . . . because we know we can! It ousts the voices that say we can't. Joy draws the heart to want to abide and persevere!

If you want to find out more of what God says about joy, go to www.blueletterbible.org and do a search on the word "joy". It will show you every Scripture with the word *joy* in it.

Joy is such a strong part of God's nature and Kingdom that He even warned Israel that their enemies would gain victory over them if they didn't serve the Lord with a glad heart. Why? Because sorrow, heaviness and complaining were a sign of unbelief and not trusting Him! Sadness and grumbling is a picture of living outside His presence. Jesus came to *rend* the spirit of heaviness and give gladness!

God is a joyful, laughing God (Ps. 2:4). Laughter is the most intense form of joy that releases healing to the spirit, soul, and body. It releases endorphins, a chemical ten times more powerful than the pain-relieving drug morphine, into the body with the same exhilarating effect as doing strenuous exercise. Laughing increases oxygen intake, thereby replenishing and invigorating cells. Statistics show that the average pre-schooler laughs or smiles four-hundred times a day. That number drops to only fifteen times a day by the time people reach age thirty-five.

I think someone needs to learn to laugh again!

The Father wants His children to love, live, and laugh . . . it's not just a slogan. After all, He does.

**"A joyful heart is good medicine, but a broken spirit dries up the bones"**—King Solomon (Prov. 17:22). God's presence restores our joy and heals our bones so that we can run the way of destiny.

## FIXING YOUR EYES ON THE PRIZE

 Satan will use anything to get us to stop us drinking deeply, and continually, from the presence of God. To quit. To drink from another well. It's easy to lose vision in a world laden with distractions and diversions, to compromise the full development of who we are in God without even realizing it. We must keep our eyes on Christ and our call to be His body for the healing of the nations.

Remember how we learned earlier that God sows with a vision for the harvest He wants? That His vision of us is that we look *fully* like the Son—full of glory and clothed in the power of the Spirit? Well, God knows our need to have a clear vision, too, of our identity in Him. And not just an initial revelation of Him and the plan He has for us; but a clear picture set before us, with our eyes fixed on Him, not forgetting what He shows us.

God spoke to His people through the prophet Habakkuk saying, **"Write the vision, and make it plain on tablets, that he may run who reads it"** (Hab. 2:2 NKJV).

See it. Write it. Run after it . . . after Him! Don't stop. Don't compromise. Don't quit. Don't get weary. Don't settle for less. Don't let the spirit of the world undermine your identity in Christ, your gifts and talents, and the fruit intended to come from your life. For surely it will try!

## THE PICTURE ON THE WALL

Let me share a brief experience and exercise that helped me years ago to run with vision. The exercise I did is one that can be applied to any aspect of our life that needs developing.

As I said before, as a young person I had a much neglected garden. My identity in Christ was being choked and overrun with weeds and thorns, and with the love of the world. I had embraced a picture of myself sketched through negative circumstances and other's perspectives. I also had a picture of my life that my flesh and the world had painted for me. Now this one looked so satisfying and dazzling. But once conformed to these images, I realized it was not who God created me to be! I was wild, rebellious, self-centered, and full of self-pity. And I was in a pit of despair. I had accepted Christ as my Savior when a child, and there was a very real seed of God within me crying out for nourishment . . . and it wanted to grow! But my identity as Abba's daughter was sitting in the dark, malnourished, crying for help.

And God heard my cry.

He put me in a place where I was surrounded with godly people who spoke encouragement into my life. But I knew that no matter how much they tried to help, the growth had to take place inside me. I needed to have a vision, *a clear picture*, of who I was as God's daughter—not who I was "going to be," but who I was, regardless of my then current stage of development. I felt so far from an identity in Christ because my thinking was muddled with myriad worldly and wounded messages. God placed me in the care of some missionaries in Argentina, and as I observed their lives and intimate relationship with God, a faith stirred inside me. I thought: *I want to know God like they do. If they can walk with Him in such intimacy, perhaps I can, too.* Their faith and love became my tangible picture of what I desired in relationship with God—a picture of a fully developed "seed" that isn't mixed with the spirit of the world.

So here's what I did. Seeing a church bulletin that had a picture of their family, I cut it out and taped it to my wall beside my pillow. Every morning and night, I saw the picture and it inspired me to press into God with fresh passion. Why? Because I knew that they didn't get to the place where they were (spiritually) overnight or by random choices! They had one focus—to know God intimately and to make Him known. They lived a lifestyle of loving God's presence and a delight to co-labor with Him in His purposes.

Seeing them, I understood that my freedom and development could only come through an intimate and deliberate relationship with God. One morning, I happened to read Jeremiah 29:13, **"You will seek Me and find Me, when you search for Me with all your heart."** I could hear the voice of God in those words, and a fresh faith gripped me. I became convinced that if I sought Him *with all my heart,* I *would* find Him. And in finding Him, I would know His glory and find true life and deliverance from my darkness. *That* was the destiny I wanted. That was my identity. I began to understand that the deceptive bondage the world offered me had been an illusory substitute.

So I started to put into practice what I saw them model and do, and what the Holy Spirit was speaking to my heart. I spent time every day in prayer, drawing close to God; I spent time praising and singing worship to Him. I studied and meditated in the Word as much as I could; I asked the Holy Spirit to give me understanding, to change my heart and conform me to the likeness of Christ. I asked Jesus to reveal Himself to me, and to show me the places in my heart that had wandered away from Him. And He led me into true repentance. I pursued the transformation of my heart to be a place of devotion to One—to Jesus. To know Him became the one cry of my whole heart until it pushed every other false lover out, until He was my supreme affection.

Those missionaries were the closest thing to Jesus that I knew, and their fully developed and fruitful lives in God inspired me as a young Christian toward a mature, authentic God-given destiny. The picture on the wall spoke a message to me—that people *can* know God intimately. And I wanted to be one of those people. The three years I spent under their ministry learning intimacy with God changed my life completely.

We need those models as we start our journey on the path of life. But the day came that I took down that picture because the image of Christ Himself was now engraved on my heart. Others pointed the way until Christ alone was my vision. Paul who said to the Corinthians, **"Be imitators of me, just as I also am of Christ,"** also said to the Ephesians, **"Be imitators of God, as dear children"** (1 Cor. 11:1; Eph. 5:1). We are all at different stages of maturity, but our goal is one—Jesus Christ. Paul nurtured intimate relationship with Christ. He *ran* after the Prize! He wanted them to do the same.

Not everyone needs to put a picture by their bed, but at the time, it was my way of "writing the vision" so I could run after it.

However, maybe there is a picture that you need to put on your wall, a verse to put on your bathroom mirror, or a specific reminder you need to put on your refrigerator. Whatever it looks like for you, get a clear picture of what your identity in Christ looks like in its mature stage. Keep it before your eyes. Keep HIM before your eyes.

Let your vision be first, and foremost, passionate intimacy with Christ. Ask the Holy Spirit to show you what that looks like for you—including how you spend your time and activities. Then, let the picture also include the natural abilities, interests, spiritual gifts and prophetic words that He's given you that need to be developed in your life—abilities and gifts that the Holy Spirit wants to flow through you in career and ministry, or prophetic insights and strategies that He wants you to fully engage. Understand that this is not who you *are* "going to be," but the seed within you of who you are that needs nourishing to *full* fruitfulness. Take special note of any reoccurring thought, dream, or prophecy to help you clarify the seed you need to develop.

Your picture may look like an influential Christian business-person, a prophetic artist, or a gifted teacher whose life touches their students with the anointing and power of God's presence. Once you understand your own spiritual identity, you still need to understand your natural abilities and call from God. For me, I had a passion for God and a desire to write and teach since I was a child. But it took many years before I realized that these gifts and passions is how God made me—for a purpose. His purpose. And that it was seed that needed cultivating in my life.

Our identity is so multi-faceted, thus our full development will be unique to each one of us. But the one thing we all have in common is the same Spirit who dwells in each of God's children. We drink from the same well of Christ's presence for full development in His image.

## THE WATER OF YOUR WORDS

Scripture says that God's presence is like rain to the garden of our heart. It also says that we can create an atmosphere of God's presence (that advances our growth) by the words of our mouth, and not just through praise, but through faith-filled words. We are created in the image of God whose words are power. Our words have power, too, and with them we declare our own prosperity, or demise.

**"Death and life are in the power of the tongue, and those who love it will eat its fruit"**—Solomon (Prov. 18:21).

Pastor Bill Johnson, author of the well known book, *When Heaven Invades Earth*, teaches that *what we sustain in our conversation, we maintain as our reality.*  What are we sustaining in our conversation? Faith? Unbelief? Edifying words? Negative words? Our words create an atmosphere around us.

One of the things Jesus practiced was speaking and naming His identity. Listen to what He says: **"I am the Bread of Life. I am the Way, the Truth, and the Life. I am the Light."** We, too, can declare our identity, watering the seed within us by naming it. We can start by repeating what HE says of us: "I am light, I am Abba's child, I am the Bride of Christ, I am a fruitful tree, I can do all things through Christ who strengthens me."

It can also include things like: I am an anointed teacher; I am a prophetic inventor, I am a successful business person; I am a prosperous Kingdom artisan. Really? Don't you think that's a little arrogant? Not really. What if I said, "I'm such a failure." Or how about, "I can't do anything". Would that be okay to say? No! But how many DO say those things? Even the world understands the power of speaking our identity. And God started it! He knows who He is and He declares it. We need to do what God does—what Father and Jesus do.

Declarations clarify and reinforce truth in our own thinking. Negative declarations carry power to kill, just as positive words carry power to energize life. When we say things like: I'm so stupid, I'm not liked, I'm a failure, I'm not wanted, and things like that, it releases a negative power over our life. As they say: **change your heart, change your *words*, change your thinking—it will change your life.**

But let me clarify, it's not just *positive* words we are to use (though positive words are important, too), but we need to declare the Word that God has spoken and written to us. He says, **"Let the Word of Christ dwell in you richly in all wisdom"** (Col. 3:16a). His words need to saturate us down to the cellular level: spirit, soul, and body. When *His* words are sustained in our *speech*, they will be maintained in our thoughts, actions, and choices, too. This will speed along our development in Him and in who we are. And I don't mean going around religiously spitting out Scripture all the time, I mean living His words, thinking like He thinks, speaking divine authority and wisdom over every situation, rather than hopeless jargon. It's called *practicing* truth, applying it, and being intimate with God's word to us. How novel is that for a Christian!

One more important note on this matter: In the O.T., God commanded Joshua to be courageous, to walk boldly in his identity as a leader who *possessed* divine promise; God also told him that success could only be achieved in this matter as long as Joshua kept the Word of God in his mind and mouth . . . CONTINUALLY! The very word *"possess"* (Heb. *"Yarash"*) comes from three word pictures: the hand, the head, the teeth. **What we take hold of, think on, and speak will cause us to possess our destiny and bring the seed we have to harvest.**

Jesus Himself modeled this for us. His response to the lure of Satan to draw Him into independence from God was, **"It is written. . . . It is written. . . . It is written!"** In other words, "Father says! Father says! Father says!" Identity is strengthened by a tongue in unity with God.

As priests of God's Kingdom we are to declare life and blessing: over our health, finances, relationships, work, talents, gifts, families, communities, and leaders. It's part of exercising dominion.

## KNOW WHO YOU ARE

Your intimacy with God, along with your spiritual gifts and natural abilities are the channels *through* which the life of the Spirit will flow to touch, edify, and impact the world around you. Your God-given talents, anointed with the Spirit, are given to you to shape communities and mold cultures. As Dr. Lance Wallnau of *Lance Learning Group* teaches, God's children are spiritual rulers to *influence* the shapers and decision-makers of the earth so that earth reflects the dominion of heaven. How? By prospering in our identity in Christ!

In 1 Corinthians 12, Paul said that if you have a gift to sing, then sing! Get good at it. Write the vision. Get educated in it. Immerse yourself in that field. Don't think too highly of yourself, but don't belittle your gift either. Let God use it! Let the Holy Spirit open doors for you. If hospitality, then practice that! Become good at it, whether on a personal level or career level. If you have a business mind, then be an entrepreneur—ask the Holy Spirit for ideas and inventions from the throne room. If it's leadership, then practice leading. Seek leadership opportunities. Learn. Grow. Give. Don't wait to have a platform, be like Joseph and be a godly leader even if it's in a prison house.

Paul continued saying that if your gift is to serve, then serve. If prophecy, then prophesy. If miracles, then stop sitting in front of the T.V. and labor with the Lord of Harvest for the healing of nations (I threw in the part about the T.V., not Paul). Learn the ways of the Spirit. Seek fellowship in your field. Don't be a loner. We aren't made to be Lone Ranger's. Be accountable and be a steward with what God has given you. And don't wait for a man's license to validate your gift. Practice who you are and let His seed in you be fruitful!

I was visiting a friend's home recently whose five year old daughter loves to dance around the church during worship times. Her actions are not only an expression of her simple love for the Lord, but it's an expression of her DNA—her passion and ability. As she stood before me twirling, I asked if she was *going to be* a dancer when she grew up. She looked up at me and declared, "I *AM* a dancer!" She already had a clear picture of her identity.

We must know who we are in every way—spiritually and naturally . . . and who we are not! Your gift and talents are not mine, and mine aren't yours. Each of us is unique, special, and needed. We are a body working together by one Spirit for one purpose—the Father's. When we understand and appreciate who we are, then striving and envy are no longer an issue. When we celebrate who we are, we can freely celebrate another with no sense of competition, because we know that we are a member of a Body that is supplying, by the Spirit, something needed for the benefit of another, not for the glory of ourselves.

## RUN TO WIN!

Father God wants you to succeed in how He designed you—not earthbound by how worldly cultures, negative environments, or wrong religious training has, perhaps, shaped you. The problem with many sons and daughters of God is that they don't know who they are. They don't know the full DNA they carry naturally and spiritually. Religion has taught us one thing. Culture has taught us another. But God's Word holds a clear picture of who we are as the anointed ones who are to bring healing to the nations, raise the dead, heal the sick, and cast out demons. We are ministers of reconciliation, rebuilders of the damaged, restorers of the devastated, repairers of what is ruined, renewing desolate generations (Isa. 61). And we are to do this right where we are—as business people, military personnel, artists, educators, and home-makers.

We are good-news bearers, oppression-breakers, broken-heart binders, freedom and favor proclaimers, gladness givers, and comfort carriers. We care for widows, orphans, and the needy. We stop human trafficking, help the addict to recover, and halt the practice of abortion, euthanasia, and abuse: physical, verbal, sexual, racial, and spiritual—because we value people. Father values people. We are *culture transformers* through truth in education, media that edifies, family units that are supported, and as creators of earth-friendly products and inventions. We turn ordinary businesses into centers of blessing . . . because we care. Because we love. Because He loves.

We have only begun to see who we are (not "going to be" someday) as children in the image of the Son—the *Ruler*—who has all dominion over *every* kingdom—the natural kingdoms and spiritual kingdoms unseen by the eye of flesh, but known by the spirit.

**"What is man that You take thought of him, and the son of man that You care for him? Yet You have made him a little lower than God, and You crown him with glory and majesty! You make him to rule over the works of Your hands; You have put all things under his feet"** (Ps. 8:4-6).

Jesus had dominion over earth's elements, spirit forces, sickness, and over His own flesh. We have been given that same authority. Jesus' intimacy with the Father gave Him an authority over all creation, seen and unseen. His intimate fellowship with the Holy Spirit empowered Him with that authority. We have been given the same intimacy with God that Jesus had. What are we waiting for?

The spirit of unbelief has taught us to live independent from the Father, and within the confines set by a natural world.

The spirit of religion has taught us to live a form of godliness without power, within the limitations set by the traditions of men.

But the Holy Spirit teaches us the truth of who God is, and who we are in Him.

All creation waits for us to understand our identity . . . and to set it free: **"For the anxious longing of the creation waits eagerly for the revealing of the sons of God . . . that the creation itself also will be set free from its slavery to corruption into the freedom of the glory of the children of God"** (Rom. 8:19-21).

No wonder the god of this world seeks the fruit of our life to snatch, scorch, and strangle it—a god who is under our feet but continually seeks to be over our head! A serpent that subtly subverts and overtly suppresses us so that we lay down our weapons, believe disempowering lies, and do not live as the sons and daughters of God who are more than "mere people" and *more* than overcomers! (1 Cor. 3:3)

Paul said, **"Run in such a way that you may win!"** (1 Cor. 9:24b). Likewise, we must garden in such a way that we bear fruit. Do not neglect so great a salvation . . . do not neglect the Word of God to you!

We live in a battle for the earth and the destinies of nations. Our success and fruitfulness as God's children is Father's answer to their well-being. We must engage the voice of God and the words He has spoken to us. We must roar with them! We must cultivate them, speed them on their way! Stop predators. Oust the intruders traipsing over our calling. Uproot the inappropriate seed making our garden unproductive and worthless. We must stand up and expose the unfruitful deeds and seeds of darkness rather than participating with them (Eph. 5:11).

One good seed watered with faith can become an innumerable blessing to the world—look at Abraham. . . . Look at Jesus!

One bad seed allowed to succeed can destroy destinies, even nations—look at Hitler.

## LOVE IS THE MARK OF MATURITY

Paul said that we can do a lot of things in life, but if we don't love, we are nothing. We are just clanging symbols. While our gifts and talents may differ, one special thing marks us as a people who carry the life of God in our identity, and that is His love.

**"By this all men will know that you are My disciples, if you have love for one another"**—Jesus (John 13:35).

Just as mature fruit has a distinct color or texture, so the expressed nature of love is the "texture" of spiritual maturity in our walk and gifts. Fear, jealousy, divisions, as well as slacking in our labor in the field with God are marks of being immature in love.

As we abide in the love of God, His love will texture our words with divine authority, our ministry with power, our character with patience, our lips with kindness, and our hands with good works. It will beam from our face with joy, our presence with peace, and it will wrap our responses toward people with gentleness and self-control. Love is the mark of maturity when our life, attitudes, gifts, and talents reflect the nature of God's own heart.

Love that moves with authority to rescue people, cultures, and nations from destruction, and bring them into life, is what the seed of His Word looks like at full development in us.

Paul, who said, **"Pursue love . . . the greatest of these is love,"** also said, **"I have fought the good fight, I have finished the course, I have kept the faith"** (2 Tim. 4:7). Paul kept faith flourishing in his life because he kept first-love alive and *first*. Thank God for the Holy Spirit who continually pours the love of God into our heart, for on our own, we could never do this without Him.

Our journey is one of many trials and encounters with an enemy who is seeking the fruit of our identity in Christ. But we have been given power and authority over him, and over sin. These no longer have *dominion* over us (Rom. 6:14). Satan wants to be ruler of this earth, but it's not given to him, but to us who are in Christ. Are we going to co-labor with Jesus for the healing of the earth? If so, then we need that good soil that listens to God, holds to what He says, and perseveres in love to bear fruit with leaves for their healing.

**"But the goal of our instruction is love from a pure heart, and a good conscious, and a sincere faith"**—Paul (1 Tim. 1:5).

## LAB CLASS: ABIDING IN LOVE THAT PERSEVERES

Write down the picture of your destiny. Write down what may be choking it. What does wisdom say you need to do to nurture its full development?

**What the Vision looks like:** _____

**What is hindering it:** _____

**What I need to do:** _____

**Here are some important questions to consider as you do this exercise:**

- What are you sensing in your spirit from the Lord as you spend time in prayer?

- What are the natural abilities you need to develop? (Look at your whole life and note past and present interests: arts, music, writing, sports, business, mechanics, medical, politics, etc. What seems to be a reoccurring theme?)

- What are your spiritual gifts you need to practice? (Wisdom, faith, prophecy, discernment, communication, hospitality, healing, knowledge, giving, craftsmanship, helps, administration, apostle, prophet, evangelist, pastor, teaching—see Romans 12, 1 Cor. 12, Eph. 4.) There are spiritual gifts tests offered on-line or in books you might want to look up.

- What do you love to do? Dream about? Think about? Your passion?

- What education and training do you need?

- What priorities do you need to put in place? Where are you procrastinating?

- What worries or activities are strangling your faith and identity in Christ?

- What relationships are hindering you with a negative influence that shuts you down?

- What good relationships do you need to cultivate more?

- What is your mouth sustaining?

- What is your mind maintaining? Are you supporting the seed of your identity in God with your thought life? Or are you supporting the spirit of the world?

- What season does God have you in? Know your season and which seed needs further development now.

**Other exercises:**

- Pursue love in every opportunity. Keep thoughts, motives, words, and actions in check with the Holy Spirit—let love become a lifestyle.

- Practice joy! It's fun. Really.

- Practice declaring God's identity—(see Appendix A), saturate yourself in intimate acquaintance with the Father, Son and Holy Spirit.

- Practice declaring your identity—how God made you both naturally and spiritually, here are some examples:

  o I am a lover of God set apart for Him

  o I am anointed of the Spirit to heal the sick and raise the dead

  o I am an anointed and righteous business person

  o I carry God's presence, glory, and power everywhere I go

  o I am a joyful overcomer

  o I love people because God's love dwells in me; I care about their well-being

Pray: *Father, help me to be a faithful gardener. Help me to love You with all my heart, all my soul, and all my strength. No compromise, no containments, no fear....just a life immersed and abiding in Your love.*

**"Be fruitful, multiply, and have dominion over the earth"** – God (Gen. 1).

# 10

## THE HARVEST AND THE END-TIME

*"Then I looked, and behold, a white cloud, and sitting on the cloud was one like the Son of man, having a golden crown on His head and a sharp sickle in His hand. And another angel came out of the temple, crying out with a loud voice to Him who sat on the cloud, 'Put in your sickle and reap, for the hour to reap has come, because the harvest of the earth is ripe.'"*
*—Revelation 14:14-15*

When Adam and Eve ate from the tree of the knowledge of good and evil, man's identity was altered from ruler to slave-child in darkness. But the recovery of our God-given DNA in Christ unveils a new creation that all earth is longing to see manifest. It is longing for the sound of the Creator's voice, the Father's voice, resonating in His children, lifting the curse that has impaled and imprisoned it.

Your success and destiny is not fate. It is the outworking of your agreement with God and the revelation He gives you. James 5:7-8 says that the farmer waits patiently for the *precious* produce of the soil. God is waiting and working for the precious harvest in your life from the seed that He's given you. The earth is waiting, too, for the manifested fruit of that seed to release heaven on earth through your words, blessing, intercession, and anointed gifts and abilities. It's waiting to receive the blessing of your intimacy with God.

Tell me again, as this is so important—what is your vision? What is the ecosystem of your heart growing? What destiny will the seed of God's word and revelation to you have? Is it being understood and accepted? Or is it being strangled and suppressed? King Solomon—the wisest king ever—understood the power of having vision, and what happens when there isn't one. He said, **"Where there is no vision the people perish"** (Prov. 29:18). Some Bible translations put it this way: **"Where there is no prophetic vision (revelation), the people cast off restraint and run wild."** That is what it means to "perish".

The Father sent the Son that *none* should perish—run wild without restraint straight into an eternity of darkness (John 3:16). Our engagement with God shapes us into the wisdom of God to be displayed in the earth before all powers and rulers. THAT is being more than "mere people". What a privilege we have been given!

There are two harvests coming to fulfillment in the earth: the seed of God and the seed of the devil (a seed empowered through the self-life). One harvest will be gathered unto God, and the other to eternal fire (Rev. 14). Their fruit is evident (2 Tim. 3):

| *Fruit of the righteous* | *Fruit of the seed of sin* |
| --- | --- |
| A lover of God | Lover of yourself |
| Faithful steward of finances | Lover of money |
| Humility | Boastful and proud |
| Nurtures others | Abusive, negligent |
| Honors parents and leaders | Disobedient to parents |
| Thankful | Ungrateful |

| | |
|---|---|
| Holy | Unholy |
| Walks in love | Without love |
| Forgives offenses | Unforgiving |
| Speaks with love | Slanderous |
| A life of power | Powerless, without self-control |
| Kind | Brutal, unkind |
| Loves what is good | Lovers of evil |
| Faithful and loyal | Treacherous |
| Wise | Foolish rage |
| Selfless | Conceited |
| Loves God more than self | Lovers of pleasure rather than lovers of God |
| Godly with power of the Spirit | Having a form of godliness but denying its power |

The choices we make either empower the divine seed within us, or they seal a devilish fate.

Sow with a vision to righteousness. Listen to God, accept what He says, and don't compromise. Bear the fruit you were born to bear. As James 2:22 tells us, our faith isn't complete until we take action on what Father says.

Your success and mine in learning Father's ways to bring about fruitfulness, means the liberation of the soul of our families, communities, and all creation—freeing them from the claws of the devourer. **It means bringing heaven's provision to earth. It means authority over weather patterns, over sickness, over demonic**

**influence and control. The flourishing of God's seed in us and our identity in Him results in His glory covering the face of the earth.**

Jesus is coming back for a people who are the revelation of Him in the earth—faithful lovers who reign now, and will reign with Him forever. These are the sons and daughters of God. This is so much more than what the Church has often been taught; it's more than living in a powerless form of godliness; it's more than a passive passing of time until we're taken out; rather, it's a return to original Divine intent for us to govern the earth realm as we live in the power of the Word and demonstration of the Spirit.

What has God given you? What call, talent, gift, idea? Will you nurture it through the growth stages until it comes to full harvest in your life? Will you guard it from the thief? From the heat of adversity? From the spirit of the world that seeks to strangle it? It is precious—treasure it! It is a living seed crying out to be nurtured. It has a destiny it wants to fulfill. The seed of the Righteous Ruler wants to rule through every aspect of who you are.

Do not underestimate what God has given you. Your success in being a fruitful son or daughter of God is what changes the world, heals its woes, and releases the needed provision from heaven to earth. The DNA within your identity in Christ is powerful, no matter how small it may seem. And if cultivated with care, it will become a rich harvest that *will* nurture others and glorify the Father in heaven.

Go. Grow your God-designed destiny. Heaven and earth are waiting for your successful journey with the Word of God inside you! Let your heart become that favorable environment for faith to flourish and gifts to prosper. Get out the repentance plow where needed. Rip out those weeds that are strangling and suffocating your much valued identity in Christ. You no longer carry the nature of a slave to sin whose identity has been stripped. You are a child of God with righteous dominion in your veins. You were born for greatness by the Great Father whose plans for you are with a bright hope, glorious future, and fruitful *today*—fruit needed for the healing of the nations.

No wonder Satan tries to stop Father's harvest in your life and mine.

Listen to God—He is speaking to you through myriad means. Hold on to what He says, accept it fully, no matter what your natural eyes see or natural mind understands. Immerse yourself in the love of Him who loves you and gave Himself for you, and remember: **it is the rich soil of your heart united with the voice and love of God that is Heaven's secret of true success— bringing the seed of your identity to full harvest.**

Christian, Christian, how does your garden grow?

# ENDNOTES

**Chapter Five: The Fate of the Withered Seedling**
Francis Frangipane, *The Three Battlegrounds*, (Cedar Rapids, IA: Arrow Publications, 2006; www.frangipane.org)

Brother Lawrence, *The Practice of the Presence of God*, (Uhrichsville, OH, Barbour Publishing 2004)

**Chapter Seven: The Fruitful Life: Hearing God**
A.B. Simpson, *Walking in the Spirit,* (Harrisburg, PA: Christian Publication, Inc.)

**Chapter Nine: The Fruitful Life: Bearing Fruit with Perseverance**
Robert Robinson, *Come Thou Fount,* (1758)

# Appendix A – Names of God

*"... but the people who know their God will display strength and take action."* (Dan. 11:32)

- **El** (Hebrew for God)—Mighty One
  Gen. 14:18; Exod. 15:11

- **I Am**—Exod. 3:14

- **Jehovah** (Heb. "Yahweh")—Gen. 2:7

- **Jehovah-jireh**—God who provides
  Gen. 22:14; Phil. 4:19

- **Jehovah-rapha**—God who heals
  Exod. 15:26

- **Jehovah-nissi**—God, my banner
  Exod. 17:15; 2 Chron. 20:17

- **Jehovah-m'kaddesh**—God who sanctifies
  Lev. 20:7

- **Jehovah-shalom**—God of peace
  Jdg. 6:24; Isa. 26:3

- **Jehovah-tsidkenu**—God our righteousness
  Jer. 23:5-6; Gal. 3:6

- **Jehovah-rohi**—God my Shepherd
  Ps. 23:1

- **Jehovah-shammah**—God who is there
  Exe. 48:35; Ps. 139:7-8

- **Almighty**—Gen. 17:1

- **Eternal God**—Deut. 33:27

- **Father of Lights**—James 1:17

- **Advocate**—1 John 2:1

- **Alpha and Omega (Beginning and the End)**
  Rev. 1:8; 22:13

- **Lord God Almighty which was, and is, and is to come**
  Rev. 4:8

- **Anointed One**—Ps. 2:2

- **Father**—Matt. 6:9, 26; Mark 14:36; Gal. 4:6

- **The Way, Truth, Life**—John 14:6

- **Judge**—Gen. 18:25

- **Living God**—Jos. 3:10

- **Bread of Life**—Jn. 6:35; 48-51

- **Compassionate & Gracious God**
  Exod. 34:6

- **Faithful and True**—Rev. 19:11

- **Forgiving God**—Neh. 9:17; Ps. 99:8

- **God of all Comfort**—2 Cor. 1:3

- **God of all Grace**—1 Pet. 5:10

- **God of Peace**—Isa. 9:6; Acts 5:30

- **God of Truth**—Ps. 31:5; Isa. 65:16

- **El-Roi**—God who sees me
  Gen. 16:13

- **God who avenges**—Ps. 94:1

- **Great & Powerful God**—Neh. 1:5; Dan. 9:4

- **Jealous God**—Col. 1:15

- **Loving God**—John 3:16
- **Wise God**—Rom. 16:27
- **Defender**—Ps. 68:5
- **Head**—Eph. 5:23; Col. 1:18

# Also Available from
## J. Nicole Williamson

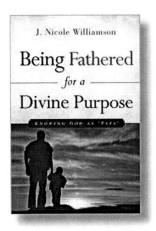

## Being Fathered for a Divine Purpose
### *Knowing God as Papa*
Experience a deeper relationship with God
Through knowing Him as your *Abba* Father
ISBN 978-1-60791-228-6


Available at
www.amazon.com or www.barnesandnoble.com
Or visit www.kingslantern.com

CPSIA information can be obtained at www.ICGtesting.com
Printed in the USA
LVOW011250111011

250019LV00001B/1/P